D0603054

SUBSTANCE
OVER
SPECTACLE

Contemporary Canadian Architecture

Andrew Gruft

with essays by
Georges Adamczyk
George Baird
Sherry McKay
Marco Polo

RETIRÉ DE LA COLLECTION UNIVERSELLE
Bibliothèque et Archives nationales du Québec

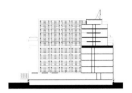

architectsALLIANCE **104**

JAMES CHENG **128**

BAIRD SAMPSON NEUERT **64**

DIAMOND AND SCHMITT **70**

BATTERSBYHOWAT **138**

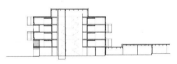

FAUCHER AUBERTIN BRODEUR GAUTHIER **38**

atelier BIG CITY **52**

WALTER FRANCL/STANTEC **166**

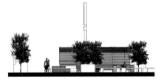

MARC BOUTIN **116**

DAN HANGANU **26**

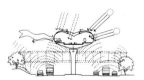

BUSBY + ASSOCIATES **170**

HENRIQUEZ PARTNERS **156**

PETER CARDEW **144**

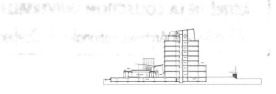

HOTSON BAKKER/KPMB **150**

KOHN SHNIER **76**

STURGESS ARCHITECTURE **112**

KUWABARA PAYNE McKENNA BLUMBERG **58**

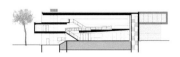

atelier TAG **32**

IAN MacDONALD **80**

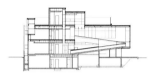

TEEPLE ARCHITECTS **98**

MacKAY–LYONS **20**

PIERRE THIBAULT **44**

PATKAU ARCHITECTS **122**

VIA ARCHITECTURE **162**

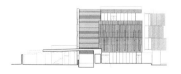

SAUCIER + PERROTTE **92**

GEORGE YU **134**

SHIM–SUTCLIFFE **86**

ACKNOWLEDGEMENTS

The production of this book and exhibition required many collaborators.

I would like to thank Scott Watson, Director of the Morris and Helen Belkin Art Gallery for his support and commitment to the project, even through difficult moments; Brian Lam and Robert Ballantyne of Arsenal Pulp Press for their willingness to take a chance on a book about Canadian architecture; the indefatigable Robin Mitchell of Picnic, our book designer, whose work with twenty-seven different architects took an enormous amount of time, energy and patience; Cindy Richmond for all her editorial attention to detail; Jana Tyner for making sense of the impossible and illegible; Owen Sopotiuk who was not fazed by the ever-expanding exhibit proposals; Annette Wooff and the staff of the Belkin—Naomi Sawada, Renée Penney and Greg Gibson—for their good humour under pressure; the writers—Georges Adamczyk, George Baird, Sherry McKay and Marco Polo—who produced thoughtful essays written specifically for this book on short notice; and those without whom there would be no exhibition and no book—all the members of the twenty-seven firms of architects, and their consultants, who design the *substance* of our Canadian architecture. I particularly wish to acknowledge the support of our donors, who generously came to our rescue at a crucial moment:

An anonymous couple

Nash Jiwa, Haywood Securities Inc.

Anthony von Mandl, Proprietor, Mission Hill Family Estate

Context Development Inc.

The Architectural Institute of British Columbia

—Andrew Gruft, Vancouver, Spring 2005

FOREWORD

As Andrew Gruft notes in his introduction, it has been eighteen years since the last survey of Canadian architecture. That survey was also curated by Gruft and mounted by this institution in its former incarnation as the University of British Columbia Fine Arts Gallery. This current publication is a more ambitious undertaking. The stakes for architecture and the institutions interested in architecture have never been higher, as an ever smaller proportion of the enormous volume of built structures are designed by architects. We argue for the critical place that architecture must occupy in any serious discussion of nation and national values; that Canadian architecture can be characterized and this is worthwhile; not in a quixotic search for a national style, but in order to assess the economic and institutional regimes that shape architectural production in this country. Our book argues for the worth and integrity of the best of Canada's contemporary architecture (of which this is not a complete survey). We hope that our country's builders will turn more and more towards architects as our cities continue to expand, and that this book will be useful to them.

The project views the Canadian situation from a Vancouver perspective. I do not mean to imply that a West Coast aesthetic has been imposed on the entire country, but that some of the issues addressed in this book resonate particularly in Vancouver. For example, the question of a national architecture is more vexed and perplexing and perhaps more suppressed.

Recent contemporary art in Vancouver often portrays what Roy Arden calls "the brutality of the new." Vancouver artists, like Arni Haraldsson and Chris Gergley, archive the buildings of the fifties; while others, such as Ian Wallace and Vikki Alexander, picture the reflecting surfaces of curtain glass, atria and malls. Jeff Wall and Stan Douglas have given us devastating images of the urban edge and/or the particularly modern North American phenomenon of the in-between zone. The late Dennis Wheeler gave us the term "defeatured landscape" to describe urban sectors given over to transportation arteries and light industry: Jeff Wall called Vancouver's cookie-cutter cityscape a "generic city." The forces that demand the generic and even the kitsch are enormous and so overwhelming that perhaps they have to be inhabited to be overcome. The projects highlighted in this book speak of a more orderly and civilized possibility and demonstrate how thoughtful and beautiful a building can be.

Andrew Gruft's persistence in bringing this project into reality deserves commendation. I hope it is not another twenty years before a further overview of architecture in Canada is realized.

—Scott Watson, Vancouver, Spring 2005

INTRODUCTION

1. Peter Buchanan, "Back to the Future," *Canadian Architect*, vol. 39, no.3 (March 1994).

2. Some of the monographs available on Canadian architects are those on Arthur Erickson, Ron Thom, Douglas Cardinal, Diamond and Schmitt, Kuwabara Payne McKenna Blumberg, Brian MacKay-Lyons, the Patkaus, Saucier + Perrotte, and Shim-Sutcliffe.

Why does no one seem to know about Canadian architecture? Internationally or locally, it gets scant notice. Mention Dutch, Swiss or Spanish architecture and you get an informed response, but the mention of Canadian architecture elicits only lack of recognition. We have many fine architects who produce great projects, but their work attracts little attention. From the mid-sixties to the mid-seventies, during the time that Peter Buchanan rightly recognizes as its greatest period,[1] Canadian architecture was highly visible and well regarded; regularly appearing on the covers of international architectural magazines and getting much coverage in the popular press. Since then it seems to have all but disappeared from view.

After spending several semesters teaching in Barcelona, I was struck by how involved Catalans were with their architecture; how much it seemed part of everyday life, routinely discussed in the newspapers as if it were regular news but with a cultural component, and accorded the same sort of attention as any other topic of civic or political interest. Unlike Canada, architects there were as well-known as doctors, lawyers or any other members of society; they were routinely named in the press when any of their buildings were mentioned, and were regularly consulted for their opinions, not only on architecture, but on a wide range of urban and cultural matters.

The discussion of ideas about Canadian architecture seems to be curiously out of favour at present. Indeed, it would appear that it is being carefully avoided, both in current writing and in the schools. Discussions of our best contemporary architecture in the journals tend to be mainly project specific, or at best strive to situate the work amongst its peers. Books on Canadian architecture are either monographs,[2] such as the excellent series from TUNS Press, or reports of competitions, such as those for the Kitchener and Mississauga City Halls or the Waterloo Clay and Glass Gallery. Compendia like Cawker and Bernstein's *Contemporary Canadian Architecture* (1982) or Whiteson's *Modern Canadian Architecture* (1983), or historical studies such as *Toronto Modern Architecture: 1945/1968*, by Baraness *et al.* (1987) and Kalman's monumental survey, *A History of Canadian Architecture* (1994), make only peripheral reference to the problematics surrounding the issue of Canadian architecture. Most of these date from the 1980s and the last appeared more than ten years ago. Courses that deal with contemporary Canadian architecture in our schools, or even the history of Canadian architecture for that matter, are almost non-existent. And students' knowledge of Canadian architects and their buildings, apart from the latest and most fashionable work, is abysmal.

In contrast, I feel we cannot build an architectural culture by studiously ignoring the fact that our architecture is designed and built in the country we call Canada. It is difficult to situate our architecture in the international arena without an understanding of how it functions at home. The resultant work ends up exuding an anonymity that somehow drains its character and "authenticity," leaving some sort of architectural simulacrum—a generic architecture indistinguishable from any other, to which no one can relate. If we are to improve the architectural climate of Canada, we need to structure a better basis for our architectural discourse, which I believe to be a key factor in the development of a rich and innovative Canadian architecture.

I found the process of starting to think about Canadian architecture difficult. The subject seemed so broad, so undefined—immense. But eventually I began trying to layout the land; a sort of site analysis, a beginning survey of the territory that might comprise Canadian architecture. My hope was to help prepare the way, to draw some sort of map that might encourage others to venture into this relatively uncharted territory, and explore the field in more detail.

While searching out and reading what others had written on the subject of Canadian architecture—from Percy Nobbs and John Lyle, to more recent picture book introductions and exhibition catalogues—I had a strong, almost visceral reaction. Why had so much writing on Canadian architecture been so self-effacing, so apologetic, so riddled with assumed inferiority—all the worse for being a self-imposed condition? It was apparent that the situation had much to do with some sort of unconscious neo-colonial attitude; an unfortunate residue of our historical past. How is it that we architects had become so alienated from our own culture, so unconfident; both blasé and cynical about ourselves? I felt the need to raise the level of consciousness. Much of this would have to do with the promotion of our architecture. As John Ralston Saul has argued, nations which do not make every effort to export their cultures are naïve and self-destructive.

Slowly my general goals became clear. I wanted to raise the profile of Canadian architecture. I wanted to try to formulate the field; to conceptualize contemporary Canadian architecture and set out a preliminary but comprehensive sketch of the surrounding issues. I hoped to develop a strategy for approaching these issues and a persuasive argument as to why such work is worth doing, and indeed, important. And last, I wanted to recuperate the currently unpopular and depreciated idea that it was possible to do serious work on national architectures, which seemed far too important a unit for the analysis of cultural difference to be abandoned because

3. I have not included a number of well-known architects, such as Arthur Erickson or Moshe Safdie, as they are part of a previous generation, the "late modernists" of the sixties and seventies.

4. *Vancouver*: Acton Ostry, Nigel Baldwin, Forsyth + McAllen, Helliwell + Smith · Blue Sky, Hughes Condon Marler, mcfarlandGreen, Pechet and Robb, Bing Thom. *Victoria*: Frank D'Ambrosio. *Calgary*: John Brown, Down + Livesay, Andrew King, McKinley Burkhart Taylor. *Edmonton*: Manasc Isaac, Barry Johns. Winnipeg: DIN, Herb Enns, Syverson Monteyne. *Toronto*: Brown and Storey, Farrow Partnership, Ralph Giannone, Hariri Pontarini, Kongats Architects, Lett/Smith, Maclennan Jaunkalns Miller, Natale and Scott, 3rd Uncle. *Ottawa*: IKOY. *Montréal*: Affleck + de la Riva, atelier Build, Atelier In Situ, Bosses, Croft Pelletier, Gauthier Daoust Lestage, LeMoyne Lapoint Magne, Marosi Troy, MEDIUM, Pierre Morency, N.O.M.A.D.E., L,O.E.U.F., Saia Barbarese Topouzanov. *Québec City*: Anne Carrier, Jacques Plante. *Halifax*: Niall Savage. *Whitehorse*: Kobayashi + Sedda.

of political misuse. If this work was successful it could be useful in helping develop a conceptual framework for the study of contemporary architecture, and at the very least it would provide some stimulus for the currently moribund discussion of architecture in Canada, which urgently needs some structure and focus to revive.

This exhibition makes a modest start in that direction. Its intent is to take a critical look at the state of contemporary architecture in Canada by assembling a representative group of projects by architects spread across the country, giving a brief overview of architectural practice. The show presents buildings by some of the "best and brightest" designers of the last ten years. It includes the work of twenty-seven architects, often working in association with others.[3] The selection of exhibitors allows a comparison of the work of the most established, serious architects with that of less established, younger architects, to see how these are developing or challenging their practice.

Seven of the architects in this show participated in *A Measure of Consensus*; the last exhibition to examine the state of Canadian architecture, which I organized and curated in 1986, and to which this show is a successor (Baird Sampson Neuert, Cardew, Cheng, Diamond and Schmitt, Hanganu, Henriquez, and the Patkaus). An eighth, (Kuwabara Payne McKenna Blumberg), is the direct descendant of a previous participant (Barton Myers Associates). Taken together with another half-dozen participants in the show, they would now form the core group of the most established serious architects in the country.

Then there are the so-called "young" (and still younger) architects. Young in the culture of architecture does not necessarily refer to the architect's age, but rather the maturity and development of their practice, something that takes many years to establish in this recalcitrant field. It is always hard to select participants for this type of exhibition, and pare down the number of architects to keep the show from becoming unwieldy, while maintaining sufficient coverage for the selection to adequately represent the whole country. But it is most difficult to choose from this younger, less-established group, where there are many more contenders of relatively equal merit. These often have insufficiently mature practices to be able to fairly judge their architectural design potential. In the end, the choice must be made, for better or worse, forced by project deadlines. The fact is that any one of another dozen firms of equivalent merit could just as easily have been included. A list of architects not in the show, but whose work deserves attention is appended.[4]

Each participant is represented by an exhibit of his or her own design and construction. This presents a single project or shows a group of related designs. These installations take a large variety of forms, but all are meant to demonstrate the architectural ideas embedded in the project or important to the architect's practice; they may include photographs, drawings or models. The idea of the self-designed exhibit is intended to help overcome the difficulty of representing architecture in the museum; it allows an actual work of the designer, albeit a modest one, to be present in the show, representing major work elsewhere.

Projects are arranged in the book crossing Canada from east to west. Starting on the Atlantic Coast, Brian MacKay-Lyons shows a set of three houses, all of which function as landscape viewing instruments and manifest the architect's search for a contemporary expression developed from the local vernacular. Two other firms are represented by private houses. Ian MacDonald shows three projects that explore the relationship of building to site at varying scales and conditions—these include an unjustly losing competition entry for the Canadian Ambassador's residence in Berlin. BattersbyHowatt, one of the "youngest" practices shown, exhibit three residential projects at increasing scale: a single-family house, their own live/work duplex, and a multi-storey fourplex. All three buildings demonstrate the use of a renewed minimal, modernist aesthetic, achieved by careful detailing within modest means.

Private houses have traditionally been used by architects as vehicles for architectural experimentation, and by young architects as a means for establishing their practice.[5] Many other architects in the show have also built fine houses. Two firms are especially renowned in this field, but are represented in this exhibition by larger works: the Patkaus and Shim-Sutcliffe. Fortunately, their residential projects are well covered by the various monographs that have been published on their work.[6]

Kenneth Frampton once commented during a visit to Vancouver that he thought the level of commercial housing here was amongst the best he had ever seen, and two firms demonstrate this through the range of projects they have built over the last dozen years. James Cheng and architectsAlliance represent the wave of commercial high density, high-rise housing that has been built in Canada over the last few years as part of the move toward living in the city centre—a trend that has improved the quality of life in Canadian cities immeasurably. Though formally disparate, both demonstrate a high standard of design and detail that is all too rare within the confines of developer driven market housing.

5. Two recent books give a better overview of the range of work in the field, see: Christine Macy, John Ota, Marco Polo, David Theodore, *Living Spaces: 21 Contemporary Canadian Homes* (Cambridge, ON: Cambridge Galleries, 2004); and George Adamczyk, *Houses-places: contemporary Canadian architecture* (Montréal; Centre international d'art contemporain de Montréal, 2004).

6. See: *Patkau Architects: Selected Projects, 1983-1993*. Brian Carter, ed. (Halifax, NS: TUNS Press, 1994); *Patkau Architects*. Andrew Gruft, intro. (Barcelona: Editorial Gustavo Gili, S.A., 1997); *Shim-Sutcliffe: The 2001 Charles & Ray Eames Lecture*. Michigan Architectural Papers 9 (Ann Arbor, MI: University of Michigan, 2002).

In response to the high cost of rental accommodation there has been a spate of student housing built on campus recently, and two projects are included here. One by Baird Sampson Neuert, a firm that has built several residences for the University of Toronto, is characterized by thoughtful aggregations of housing units into clean, modern collegiate buildings of residential scale. The other by Eric Gauthier of FABG is for performers at the Cirque du Soleil, where the expression of individual housing units is used to great sculptural effect. The project contributes to the excellent collection of new buildings now to be found on the site in north Montréal, which includes the original buildings by Dan Hanganu and a new circus school by LeMoyne Lapointe Magne.

Taken as a group, these residential projects give some idea of the range and strength of housing construction in the country. No examples of classic "social housing" are included, because much less has been built in recent years due to cuts in government funding, as a result of the rightward shift in Canadian politics.

Since the sixties, when projects like Arthur Erickson's Simon Fraser University and John Andrews' Scarborough College set the standard for innovative architecture in Canada, universities have been amongst the most enlightened patrons of good design. In some provinces, this tradition has sadly disappeared, as control over development has foolishly been surrendered to project managers recruited from the private sector, whose only interest is the bottom line. Fortunately some institutions take their cultural responsibility more seriously, particularly in Ontario and Québec, where they have continued this tradition by engaging the best architects and encouraging them to produce innovative work.

In the Child Study Centre at the University of Toronto, Stephen Teeple shows how a kindergarten can be transformed into a magic box brought alive by children's activity. At Trent University, another exemplary early campus, Teeple has built an extension to the new science complex facing Ron Thom's original buildings—a series of long fingers reach down to the river, dynamic slivers of metal and glass divided by long narrow courtyards. This idyllic setting is unfortunately marred by a recent act of architectural vandalism perpetrated on the campus by insensitive architects and an inept administration, in the form of a new student residence badly placed and out of scale, which now dominates this side of the river.

In contrast, the spate of construction at UBC through the 1990s produced few distinguished buildings. One striking exception is Peter Cardew's Morris and Helen Belkin Art Gallery—a highly expressive building that caused a stir on campus and works remarkably well as a gallery in spite of its rejection of the accepted model of the neutral white box. Its existence owes much to the support of enlightened donors and the efforts of the Director, Scott Watson, who uses the design to its best advantage. We are pleased to be able to open the exhibition in a space that manifests something of the spirit of Canadian contemporary architecture.

Two other university buildings, the Bahen Centre for Information Technology at the University of Toronto by Diamond and Schmitt, and a new campus for Concordia University in downtown Montréal by Kuwabara Payne McKenna Blumberg, are amongst the largest projects in the show. Each is about the size of a city block, and involves dealing with equivalent complexity. Both demonstrate clarity of organization and circulation critical for projects of this size, and a strong architectural expression that is varied but coherent within the overall unity of the project. In some ways these projects stand in for office buildings in the exhibition—a type that seems stuck in the mode of late modernism, and does not appear to have made much advance in Canada since the days of Mies van der Rohe's Toronto Dominion Towers.

Setting the tone for the redevelopment of an old industrial site into a civic office precinct for Calgary, Jeremy Sturgess designs the new Municipal Water Treatment Centre as a striking imagistic object that also meets the desired high level of sustainability. Kohn Shnier renovate a mundane industrial building located in the bleak *terrain vague* adjoining a major freeway into a landmark headquarters building for Umbra, a producer of stylish home furnishings. In an intervention conceptualized as "putting on a pair of sunglasses," the building is dressed up in an outfit of translucent plastic panels, demonstrating the ability of a strong and simple idea executed with flair to transform the banal into an eye-catching image of corporate identity.

Under the direction of Alan Hart, whose firm Via Architecture was entrusted with the overall architectural design and coordination of the Millennium SkyTrain Line, talented architects were commissioned to design each of the new stations. Two standouts are Brentwood by Peter Busby and Lake City by Walter Francl/Stantec, each of which interprets the strict station programme in different but equally exciting ways, contributing to an outstanding infrastructure project, extremely popular with the public and appreciated for its high level of design.

Richard Henriquez—long a proponent of such literary tropes as metaphor and narrative in his architecture—uses images abstracted from DNA, chromosomes, and even the Petri dish to infuse specific meaning into his design for the BC Cancer Research Centre in Vancouver. In a more abstract conceptual mode, Gilles

Saucier and André Perrotte use the two main façades of the Perimeter Institute for Research in Theoretical Physics in Waterloo, Ontario, to imply different facets of the institution's character, while the circulation is conceived as "crossing the improbable space between theoretical physics and everyday life."

The Québec system of awarding public building commissions by competition is much admired and envied throughout Canada, and has enabled a number of young architects to set-up and develop their practice. The two best known of these, atelier big city and atelier TAG, were founded twenty years apart, yet follow similar trajectories of development; all their projects shown here are the result of entering architectural competitions. Anne Cormier, Randy Cohen and Howard Davies of atelier big city show three public projects for rural Québec—simple and clear in concept, and rendered in their trademark populist, cartoon style. These demonstrate a design approach consistently applied across twenty years, clearly qualifying them as *auteurs* in the sense described by George Baird in his essay.

atelier TAG recently stormed the Québec scene by winning two important competitions within two years. Formally simple but conceptually strong, Manon Asselin's and Katsuhiro Yamazaki's designs proposed the Châteauguay Library as a "standing stone cabinet of books" in the city park, whereas the Théâtre du Vieux-Terrebonne is conceived as a device for seeing and being seen, with the role of spectator clandestinely transforming into that of the observed while moving through the project.

Strawberry Vale by John and Patricia Patkau, arguably the finest school built in Canada over the last fifteen years, pushes the limits of spatial complexity and expressive detailing achieved in a public institution. The design has some of the most wonderful classrooms I have ever seen; flooded with natural light, geometrically orthogonal but with the most remarkable feeling of free-form space. This innovative project became the lightning rod for a storm of ill-informed and ill-considered criticism from provincial politicians, in what should have been an enlightened social-democratic government. Particularly reprehensible was the public attack on the work of all architects by the then Minister of Education, an anti-cultural, anti-intellectual rant worthy of the most reactionary redneck.

A seamless blend of traditional and contemporary architecture, Dan Hanganu's Centre d'archives de Montréal makes an exemplary renovation of three significant historic buildings, integrated by new construction into a coherent public project on the edge of the old city. Richmond City Hall by Hotson Bakker/Kuwabara Payne McKenna Blumberg melds civic typology with the topography of the Fraser

River delta into a handsome ensemble worthy of the long tradition of fine suburban city halls built in Canada over the last three decades. Reinterpreting fifties West Coast modernism and the Pacific North-West garden tradition, they provide a contemporary civic centre for this sprawling, multi-ethnic suburb.

With few exceptions, commercial retail development is an area avoided by most serious architects since the days of the invention of the modern shopping centre by Walter Gruen in the mid-twentieth century. George Yu sets *Shop* Lift in Richmond—the Vancouver suburb renowned for its innovative shopping mall developments, which are strongly influenced by Asian consumer culture. At once a shopping, residential and recreational complex, Shop Lift envisions a consumer environment that is strategically integrated with open public spaces and private dwelling units, proposing a new hybrid form of urban development.

We are experiencing a renewed interest in the social basis of architecture, not seen since the optimistic times of the seventies. Marc Boutin shows three projects demonstrating the use of "negotiable space"—a concept that seeks to activate the public realm, and space in general, through the transformation of passive users into active participants by the design of anticipatory infrastructure.

With the design of Ledbury Park, Shim-Sutcliffe have built an outdoor community centre that provides a new neighbourhood focus, creating a new topographic condition from scratch, and integrating architecture and landscape into a beautiful and elegant series of elements that function equally well through all seasons.

Pierre Thibault is renowned for a brilliant series of poetic installations in the countryside and wilderness of Québec. This ongoing series of projects animate our perception of the landscape without permanently altering the environment, and address the blurred boundary separating nature and culture, while imaginatively inserting themselves somewhere in-between.

These projects present a broad panorama of architectural activity in Canada, giving a clear impression of its character. The scope of the selection is intended to demonstrate a typology of "architectures" that make up the field, so that the viewer might understand the range of work being produced in the country and assess its importance and viability.

Five critical essays begin to conceptualize and position architectural practice in Canada. They explore a number of key issues regarding contemporary architectural production and discuss some of the architectural ideas, formal strategies and design solutions of the work presented. I am particularly interested in revealing the underlying values, attitudes and preoccupations that predispose the work towards the specific direction it takes. As I explain in my essay, which proposes a conceptual framework for the discussion of contemporary architecture, this is especially relevant to studies that use the cultural-geographical unit of the nation state, such as Canada, as the catchment for the work to be examined.

George Baird's text explores the possibility of treating certain contemporary Canadian architects as *auteurs*, using this term in the sense employed in the history of contemporary film. Despite the fact that virtually no Canadian architects qualify as *stars* in the current international architectural milieu, Baird argues for considering them *auteurs*, which facilitates a revaluation of their work parallel to that made by French film critics and theorists in the fifties and sixties, who argued for the importance of the films of American directors such as Howard Hawks, Alfred Hitchcock and John Ford, previously considered mere journeymen.

Sherry McKay's essay looks at the ways in which ideas of Canadian architecture have shifted through history according to professional discourses and the specificities of the wider context—climate, materials, political aspirations, technology and building culture. It counters the commonly asserted opinion that, until very recently, Canadian architecture has been derivative of canonical architecture found elsewhere. As the essay reveals, these hybrid and misquoted forms, when reconsidered according to the insights afforded by contemporary cultural theory, can be understood as strategic responses to contingencies of practice and meaning. Instead of stable forms in a historical continuum, McKay proposes that Canadian architecture might be better understood as responsive traces of vital cultural processes.

Georges Adamczyk looks at the development of architecture within the context of the changes taking place in the cultural situation of Québec over the last twenty years. Set against the tension between local tradition and modernism, he outlines some of the architectural debates that took place during that time, particularly those in the pages of *ARQ*. He speculates that, perhaps influenced by the competition system of Québec, what characterizes these architects and their ideas is "l'expression de la différence."

Marco Polo's essay discusses how, over the past fifteen years, Canadian architecture has emerged from a brief flirtation with postmodern classicism to embrace a self-conscious, "mannered" modern aesthetic reflective of two divergent, but complementary models—the rational and the romantic. The essay discusses these phenomena in the context of changing conditions of practice, project procurement, the role of competitions and other cultural and socio-economic factors, and speculates on possible future directions suggested by recent developments in Canadian architecture.

Many of the characteristics of Canadian architecture have been covered in these essays. But if one were to attempt to summarize the distinguishing feature of contemporary Canadian architecture in one, perhaps overly simple statement, it would express its resistance to the spectacular and pursuit of a more balanced design approach. I would suggest that Canadian architecture would identify more with the work of a Rafael Moneo rather than that of a Will Alsop; a Herman Hertzberger rather than a Rem Koolhaas; a Renzo Piano rather than a Daniel Libeskind.

Canadian architecture has always eschewed the dominance of formalism for more complex and integrated solutions reflecting its humanist concerns. When Polo proposes the possibility of a renewed modernism based on sustainability, I would suggest that given the nature of Canadian practice, the addition of sustainability as another layer of complexity should not be difficult. As I explained in my 1986 catalogue essay:

> But the strong social-democratic tradition of governmental supervision and community control in Canada influences architecture through a complex frame-work of programming, design guidelines, zoning by-laws and building codes, within which designers must operate. Such a system is unlikely to allow stylistic concerns to override programmatic ones, making the production of radical projects more difficult than in a laissez-faire society. This seems to have challenged rather than inhibited the imagination of the designers in this exhibition, and enriched their work with a multivalent layering of response to a broad range of demands.[7]

7. Andrew Gruft, *A Measure of Consensus: Canadian Architecture in Transition* (Vancouver: University of British Columbia Fine Arts Gallery, 1986), 51.

Such values form the underlying basis of a Canadian architecture that favours substance over spectacle, distinguishing itself from the work of many other nations now garnering attention in the architectural press. The media always prefer a simplistically imagistic architecture. This means that a more subtle and complex architecture, such as that practiced in Canada, and one that cannot be read at a glance, but which requires a commitment of time and effort on the part of the viewer to understand, gets much less attention, and has a much lower profile in the international architectural arena.

8. *New Commitment: In Architecture, Art and Design* (*Reflect* #01), Foreword by Simon Franke (Rotterdam: NAi Publishers, 2003).

After many years of self-preoccupation while operating as an autonomous discipline, there are encouraging signs everywhere that architecture is again opening up to a broader range of issues in the world at large. When a leading architectural institution such as the Netherlands Architecture Institute announces a new series of publications titled *reflect*, focusing on socially relevant themes for architecture, this is clearly a debate that is already well under way. The first of these books, *New Commitment*,[8] is a collection of essays on social engagement in architecture, intended to stimulate the discussion. Canadian architects are well positioned to take-up the challenge of this complex issue, with our tradition of a practice that is accustomed to integrating a variety of often competing demands into a richer, more nuanced architecture. We also have the advantage of our history to inspire us: the precedent setting, socially conscious and adventurous work of the "sixties." Perhaps this is where the attention of Canadian architecture will shift over the next generation, once again producing work that is at the leading edge.

—Andrew Gruft

SUBSTANCE OVER SPECTACLE
Exhibitors

MacKAY–LYONS
Messenger House II
Upper Kingsburg

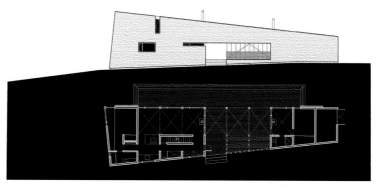

Hill House
South Shore of Nova Scotia

These three hilltop houses represent a sustained research focus from a practice that emphasizes the development of an integrated body of work under the guise of "village architect" (Design Quarterly #165). Together they offer a glimpse of the practice of MacKay-Lyons Architects, presenting three variations on the theme of building and landscape. All three houses function as landscape viewing instruments. To paraphrase Glenn Murcutt, they "reveal and amplify the cultural and natural structure of the coastal rural landscape." They objectify the captured landscape between their courtyard making forms, thereby creating a tension between their major and minor programme elements. Each responds in its own way to the archetypal desire for both prospect and refuge associated with hilltop dwelling. All three of the houses present blunt, rump-like ends outward, and more domesticated faces inward.

In Messenger House II, the court emerges as a "stretch mark" when the main and guest houses are pulled apart under one roof-form, opening up the view to 400 year old ruins below. In Hill House, the house and barn are pin-wheeled in plan so that ironically, one views the landscape by looking inward, across the garden court, and past the other structure. In House on the Nova Scotia Coast #22, both the main house and guest-house occupy two drumlin hilltops that are 400 feet apart, and framing a cultivated wildlife corridor in the valley between.

A parallel line of research investigates the area of material culture. All three projects explore the light timber framing traditions of Nova Scotia. While House on the Nova Scotia Coast #22 employs an elemental, tectonic expression, both Messenger House II and Hill House employ a monolithic expression that creates an ironically massive effect out of conventional stick frame construction.

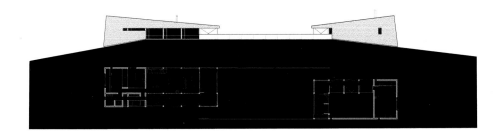

Brian MacKay-Lyons Architect Ltd.
Halifax, Nova Scotia
www.bmlaud.ca

Brian MacKay-Lyons
b. 1954, Arcadia, Nova Scotia; B.ED. (TUNS), 1976; B.Arch. (TUNS),
1978; M.Arch. (UCLA), 1982.

House on the Nova Scotia Coast #22
South Shore of Nova Scotia 1997-1998
Project Team
Rob Meyer
Bruno Weber
Marc Cormier
Structural Engineer
Campbell Comeau Engineering Ltd.
Photography
Undine Prohl
James Steeves

Messenger House II
Upper Kingsburg, Nova Scotia 2001-2003
Project Team
Trevor Davies
Chad Jamieson
Peter Blackie
Structural Engineer
Campbell Comeau Engineering Ltd.
Photography
James Steeves
Brian MacKay-Lyons Architect

Hill House
South Shore of Nova Scotia 2002-2004
Project Team
Talbot Sweetapple
Chad Jamieson
Melanie Hayne
Geoff Miller
Structural Engineer
Campbell Comeau Engineering Ltd.
Photography
Brian MacKay-Lyons Architect

DAN HANGANU
Centre d'archives de Montréal

Guardian and source of diffusion of the collective memory of our society, the Québec Provincial Archives in Montréal is responsible for the conservation of and access to documents of patrimonial value. The project consists of a new building integrating three existing buildings that were altered to form the new archive centre.

The site occupies an entire city block and each of the three existing buildings represents a significant era from recent history. Together, they present an image of disparate architectural styles and scale. The addition of a fourth building on the site, housing archival storage, transforms a left-over service yard into a central, sky-lit interior atrium. An exterior courtyard, framed by the Jodoin Mansion, is visually connected to this space.

The design emphasizes public accessibility for academics and the public; from historians and archivists to occasional visitors and tourists. The facility features a variety of spaces and utilizes transparency and natural light to convey a sense of openness throughout. It comprises a multi-storey reading room, an exhibition space, an auditorium, climate-controlled document storage areas, document repair workshops, and a café.

The architectural parti for the project is developed about the main compositional axis of the former HEC Building; its monumental colonnaded principal entrance sets the stage for the unfolding of a sequence of glorious interior spaces, culminating in the main reading room. The main entrance hall of the HEC Building, the former museum with its glass-floored mezzanines and the Jodoin Mansion, are restored to their previous architectural grandeur.

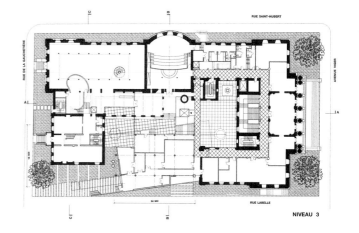

NIVEAU 3

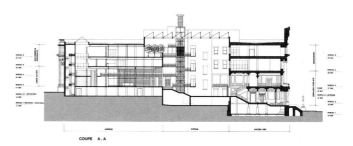

COUPE A . A

Dan S. Hanganu architectes
with Provencher Roy et associ
Montréal, Québec
www.hanganu.com

Dan S. Hanganu
b. 1939, Iasi, Romania; Dip.Arch

Centre d'archives de Montréa
Montréal, Québec 1997-2000

Project Team
Michel Roy
Gilles Prud'homme
Thomas Schweitzer
Normand Desjardins
Guillaume de Lorimier
Marie-Claude Lambert
Alex Touikan
Rejean Comeau
Michael De Angelis
Michel Amor
Structural Engineer
Les Consultants Geniplus Inc.
Mechanical, Electrical Engi
Groupe Dupras Ledoux associ
Scenography
Trizart-Alliance Inc.
Interior Design
GSM Design
Project Manager
Gespro SST
Client
Societe immobiliere du Québe
Photography
Michel Brunelle

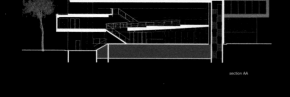

section AA

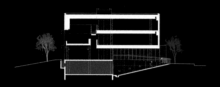

section BB

atelier TAG (technique + architecture + graphisme) is an architecture and research partnership dedicated to exploring the possibilities of architecture through a close examination of a given socio-cultural context and its specific relation to the programme. The intersection between theory and practice provides the foundation for inventive solutions to conventional and often overlooked building typologies. This approach allowed the firm to win two province wide architectural competitions: the Châteauguay Library in 2001 and the Théâtre du Vieux-Terrebonne in 2003.

The Municipal Library of Châteauguay is located in the city's civic park. Upon this landscape of green dunes, the Library appears as the city's "standing stone." Symbolically, the library's fieldstone cabinet of books levitates above the landscape and provides a new gateway to the park.

Whereas on the main street side the book collection of the new library is metaphorically contained within a hard cover of fieldstones, on the park side its cross section is revealed. This "mise en scène" of the programme transforms the inactive function of book storage into social spectacle, and promotes the role of the municipal library as communal gathering place.

The programme of the library is structured in two main strata. The ground floor is conceived as a fluid "public place" in continuity with the natural grades of the landscape. The library proper is housed on the above two floors. Ascending by a grand stair through the inclined plane of the second floor, one emerges in the double height space of the "hall oblique." Opening onto the park's canopy of trees, the vast space of this upper hall is perceived in contrast to the intense density of the two story cabinet of books. Circulating through the numerous rows of books one discovers inner courts. Conceived as clearings in a dense forest of printed material, these gardens situate the reading areas and provide framed views of the exterior landscape.

The Théâtre of Vieux-Terrebonne is also located in that city's civic park, overlooking the spectacular riparian landscape of the Mille-Îsles River. The théâtre is conceived as a monolith punctuated by enclosed gardens. The limit of the théâtre's envelope is blurred, letting the park's "flâneurs" in, and the occupants of the théâtre out. The ascending ramp of the telescopic garden traverses the mass of the théâtre from north to south, and culminates on the river. The programmatic elements are structured along this main axis. The double height foyer bridges the axis, providing panoramic views of the river, while animating the main street. The Théâtre du Vieux-Terrebonne is a device for seeing and being seen. It is conceived as a social incubator where ones' role as spectator clandestinely transforms into that of the observed.

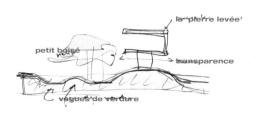

atelier TAG
with Jodoin Lamarre Pratte et Associes Architectes in joint venture
Montréal, Québec
t.a.g@videotron.ca

Manon Asselin
b. 1966, Québec City; B.Sc.Arch. (McGill), 1990; B.Arch. (McGill), 1992; MA.Hist. & Theory Arch. (McGill), 2001.
Katsuhiro Yamazaki
b. 1972, San José, Costa Rica; B.Sc.Arch. (McGill), 1994; B.Arch. (McGill), 1996.

Bibliothèque Municipale
Châteauguay, Québec 2001-2003
Project Team
Tom Yu
Marc Laurendeau
Denis Gaudreault
Michel Nantel
Julien Fantini
Olivier Millien
Sylvain Morrier
Structural, Mechanical, Electrical Engineer
Dessau-Soprin

Contractor
Gerpro Construction Inc.
Acoustics
Jean Pierre Legault Acoustique
Building Signage
Pawel Karwowski
Client
City of Châteauguay
Photography
Marc Cramer
atelier TAG

Théâtre du Vieux-Terrebonne
Vieux-Terrebonne, Québec 2002-2004
Project Team
Tom Yu
Irina Nazarova
Andrea Merrett
Marc Laurendeau
Jean Martin
Gerard Lanthier
Guylaine Beaudoin
Structural Engineer
Leroux Beaudoin Hurens et associés

Mechanical, Electrical Engineer
Nacev Consultants inc.
Landscape
atelier TAG with Céline Paradis Landscape Architect
Scenography
Trizart Alliance inc.
Acoustics
Octave Acoustique inc.
Contractor
Gerpro Construction inc
Building Signage
Pawel Karwowski
Client
Société de développement culturel de Terrebonne
Photography
S. Arbour
atelier TAG

FAUCHER AUBERTIN BRODEUR GAUTHIER

Housing for Artists

Cirque du Soleil, Montréal

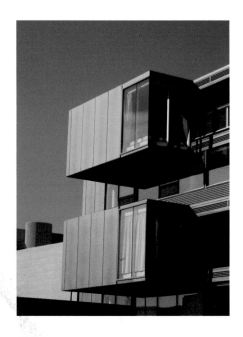 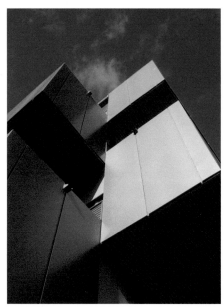 

Young artists and athletes from around the world converge on the Cirque du Soleil headquarters in Montréal for an intensive few months of training before joining the touring company. This building contains living spaces with balconies—115 studios and suites—for these performers, as well as a fitness room and an internet café. A large cube of rooms sits above a plinth of common spaces on 2nd Avenue, in front of the Cirque's headquarters, and a lower bar is aligned with the residential neighbourhood on Jean-Rivard street.

The building's expression of stacked containers alludes to the transient nature of its nomadic occupants, and the tension that exists between the individual and the collective within the company. The project explores the notion of dynamic equilibrium in the same way that jugglers, contortionists and trapeze artists play with weight to defy gravity.

Faucher Aubertin Brodeur Gauthier
Montréal, Québec
www.arch-fabg.com

Eric Gauthier
b. 1960, Québec City; B.Arch. (Québec) 1983.

Housing for Artists, Cirque du Soleil
Montréal, Québec 2002-2003

Project Team
André Lavoie
Dominik Potvin
Structural Engineer
Renaud Lapointe Ingenieur
Mechanical, Electrical Engineer
Progemes Consultants
Photography
Steve Montpetit

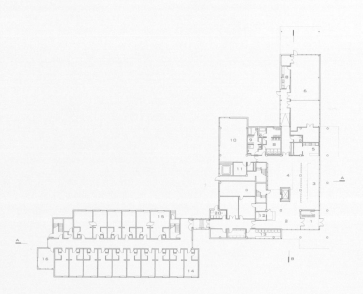

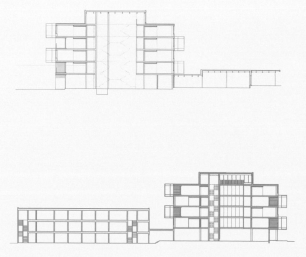

PIERRE THIBAULT
Winter Gardens

Winter Gardens reflects time as it occurs within a specific, natural landscape. The project's interventions act as fugitives: gardens of snow, ice and light come to rest softly on a ground just as impermanent—the frozen lakes of winter.

As an inquiry into space, the project seeks to modify our perception of landscape without permanently altering the environment. Using nature's own repertory in careful, deliberate ways, it addresses the blurred boundary that separates nature and culture, inserting itself somewhere between the two.

Caravan

Aligning tents across the surface of a lake strips winter camping of its discretion. Through the unbroken line of the tents, transient human presence is sublimated and the tents become either caravan or road, crossing the lake and the forest, reaching out for the horizon.

At night, the illuminated chain that results resembles an electric line slicing through the wilderness, a succession of lanterns on the ground. Progression and immobility are juxtaposed, perhaps even opposed, as the accumulated effect of numerous fixed units moves in a vibrant way through the darkness.

Constellation

At night in winter, the frontier that separates the lake from its surrounding environment disappears, and only two elements remain: earth and sky. The shape of the lake is redefined by lighting two thousand candles over the entire frozen surface. For a short period of time, the lake takes on the guise of a reflected night sky, but closer, as though seen through a magnifying glass.

Icebergs

In winter, the ground and lake are both immaculately white, and any indication of water beneath the surface is extrapolative. By exhibiting raw ice shorn with regular precision and unmasking what is seasonally hidden from view, Icebergs highlight the interplay between human intervention and the natural order.

Rhapsody

Seven hundred and fifty flutes are installed in a regular grid over the entire surface of the lake. As the wind blows, air is caught in the flutes, producing a melody whose momentum varies according to the wind's strength and direction. The lake sings in the winter silence.

Floating Garden

Located on the Baie-des-Chaleurs, the project embodies a process of reflection on landscape, sensitively articulating an approach to creation that pertains to a specific place at a specific time. Staging this process of reflection has resulted in a programme composed of a number of iconic gardens that can be moved about the bay.

Floating Garden refers to gardens located on cedar platforms. Various elements, including bases, floaters, lights and screened enclosures, may be integrated within each platform. Therefore each garden assumes a unique personality, and all are highly versatile. For example, they may be "refuged" on sand, appear as spectral "islands" in the midst of the sea, or take on the guise of miniature "oases" cut loose from shore.

The Garden as Raw Material for Expression
Through the use of raw materials taken from the host landscape, and found objects that are testimonies of human intervention, the art of the garden in this context becomes an iconic expression highly representative of the Baie-des-Chaleurs:

Minerals: rocks, sand, pebbles
Plants: grasses, flowers, mosses, lichen, algae
Water: spring water, salt water
Artifacts: objects salvaged on the shore

The project is an exploration of the complementary tension that can exist between the broader natural landscape—the elements (winds, tides), the seasons, ecology, biodiversity—and artistic reflection. The inherent mobility of the gardens, and their actual location at any given time, multiplies and enhances our understanding of their nature. It is this blending of raw landscape in its "natural" and "manipulated" forms that makes it possible to create an always-renewed dialogue between what already exists and our manufactured and mediated interpretation of such.

Territory Garden

The coastal geography of the Saint Lawrence River was shaped through a long evolutionary process that produced today's rugged landscape. For the past fifty years, the Jardins de Métis has been a counterpoint to the undomesticated coast, with its varied and beautiful garden compositions, many integrating rare plants. Every year, for the length of one season, ten designers are invited to Métis to create a garden of their own.

For the 2001 edition, we imagined the Territory Garden, in which the region's geography and the shoreline's building blocks were appropriated through poetic abstraction. Water, plants and minerals were configured throughout the garden like fragments of nature removed from an original setting and relocated here. Metal defined the contours against which territory was contained. The shoreline's raw materials evoked the perennial forces that have shaped the coastal landscape. Subterfuge reinforced the sense of wonder: shoulder-high wheat densely planted throughout the entire garden hid the sliced fragments of territory from immediate view. The tall yellow stalks beckoned visitors to the adventure of discovery. Senses were heightened.

Pierre Thibault architecte
Québec City, Québec
www.pthibault.com

Pierre Thibault
b. 1959, Montréal; B.Arch. (Laval) 1982.

Winter Gardens (Frozen lake)
Parc des Grands-Jardins, Québec 2000-2004
Project Team
Vadim Siegel
Katerine McKinnon
Charles Ferland
Jean-François Mercier
Anaïs Corbier
Client
Parc des Grands-Jardins
Photography
Pierre Thibault

Floating Garden (Jardins sur la Baie)
New Richmond, Québec 2003
Project Team
Thibaud Foucray
Katerine Mc Kinnon
Charles Ferland
Jean-François Mercier
Client
City of New Richmond, Gaspésie
Photography
Pierre Thibault

Territory Garden (Jardins de Métis)
Grand-Métis, Québec 2001
Project Team
Vadim Siegel
Katerine Mc Kinnon
Client
International Garden Festival, Redford Gardens, Jardins de Métis
Photography
Pierre Thibault

atelier BIG CITY
Centre d'interpretation du Bourg de Pabos.
Chandler

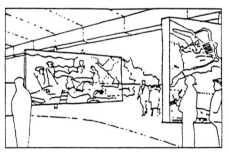

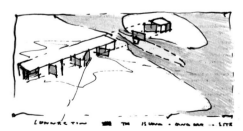

Parc de l'aventure basque en Amerique
Trois-Pistoles

Competition Entry for
Théâtre du Vieux-Terrebonne

 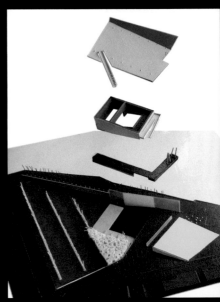

In our work there has always been a desire for continuity between building and landscape—our designs attempt to push the very form of the architecture into a more fundamental and experiential relationship to its site. Topography, wherever possible, is folded into constructed form and sectional manipulations. Tree growth, clearings and water are brought into the project in an analogous fashion to programmatic components. The intention is the comprehensive utilization of both natural and constructed forms towards the clear and generous articulation of the conceptual project. In many instances the landscape project is programmed by either functional or symbolic means—users are made to traverse a section of landscape as a programmed event. Such programmed events are fundamentally tied to the project's ideological and formal intentions. Through this process the project takes on an experiential and symbolic connection to its site that is never arbitrarily imported, but rather organically and incrementally generated.

In Pabos, the building is made a vehicle for interpretation. A structure comparable to a giant exhibition stand is installed on the point of land. The transformable walls of the structure open outward to the landscape in the summer and contract in winter, allowing the structure to close in on itself. The history of Pabos is superimposed on its landscape; images evoking this history are reproduced on pivoting perforated panels. The structure is a "machine for seeing." More than one narrative is possible.

For the Basque Interpretation Centre at Trois-Pistoles, the continual unfolding of discovery through the visitor's promenade is used as a way of structuring the various functional requirements of the programme. The siting and articulation of the elements propose a strategy of projections of various scales (mise en abime). The building acts as a constructed landscape—its shape and siting create a sheltered exterior enclave. Like a section of landscape, its form is continuous and flowing, wall to roof, roof to wall and wall to playground.

The riverside site of the Terrebonne théâtre, near a collection of significant historic structures, provided the inspiration for a design strategy that proposed merging the théâtre with an inclined park space. The demand for surface parking was integrated in this strategy of carving and shaping the "good" earth of Terrebonne to create a dynamic urban space that was both symbolic and ecological.

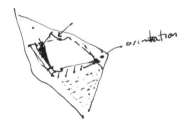

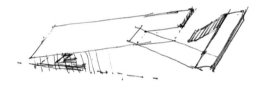

atelier big city
Montréal, Québec
www.atelierbigcity.com

Anne Cormier
b. 1959, Montréal; B.Sc.Arch. & B.Arch. (McGill) 1982; C.E.A.
Architecture Urbaine (Paris) 1987.
Randy Cohen
b. 1958, Toronto; B.Sc.Arch. & B.Arch. (McGill) 1982;
Grad. Dip. Architectural Theory (London) 1986.
Howard Davies
b. 1959, Montréal; B.Sc.Arch. & B.Arch. (McGill) 1982.

Centre d'interprétation du Bourg de Pabos
Chandler, Québec 1991-1993
Project Team
atelier big city
Archaeological Research
Ethnoscop inc.
Les Recherches Arkhis inc. under the direction of Pierre Nadon
Structural Engineer
Kumar Maldé
Electrical, Mechanical Engineer
Yvon Plante et Associés inc.

Landscape
Le Groupe Lestage inc. (Claude Cormier)
Contractor
Les Constructions Vision 2000 inc.
Interpretation Coordination
atelier big city
Researcher
Louise Pothier, Archaeologist
Animation
Marie-Thérèse Bournival
Graphic Design
Associés Libres
Client
La corporation du Bourg de Pabos
Sponsors
Ministère de la Culture du Québec
Federal Bureau of Regional Development
Le Secrétariat général aux affaires régionales (SGAR)
Photography
Raymond Garrett
Michel Laverdiere
atelier big city

Parc de l'aventure basque en Amerique
Trois-Pistoles, Québec 1994-1996
Project Team
atelier big city
Structural, Mechanical, Electrical Engineers
Sopax inc.
Landscape
Claude Cormier
Contractor
Marcel Charest & Fils
Client
Le Centre international du loisir culturel de Trois-Pistoles
Photography
atelier big city

Competition Entry for Le Théâtre du Vieux-Terrebonne
Terrebonne, Québec 2002
Project Team
atelier big city
Ecological Consultation
Danny Pearl
Mark Poddubiuk
Landscape Design
Patricia Lussier
Anna Radice

KUWABARA
PAYNE
McKENNA
BLUMBERG
Le Quartier Concordia
Montréal

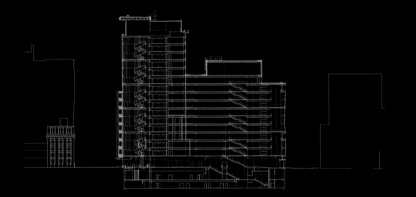

The absence of a historic campus fabric created an opportunity to remake Concordia's image from a loose aggregate of buildings within downtown Montréal into an identifiable urban precinct. The faculties of Engineering/Computer Science (ENCS) and Visual Arts (VA), and the John Molson School of Business (JMSB) are organized into three respective buildings that occupy two city blocks. The complex is conceived as a vertical campus to accommodate the multi-departmental programmes within the limited footprint, and sited to define a threshold between the city and university. The vertical campus is symbolized by stacked atria containing spiral stairs that facilitate circulation between floors, and create zones for interaction between students and faculty.

The concept creates a family of distinct, yet related architectural forms. The overall composition is unified by a series of figurative canopies that project off the roofs of each building, while the elevations of each building are differentiated to express its specific function and orientation. The VA building is articulated by a large-scale grid, using sill to ceiling glass with operable windows, expressing a robust loft. The ENCS and JMSB buildings are tauter and vertically expressed to reflect the secretarial nature of the programmes within. The base of each building is scaled to pedestrians, and draws the space of the street deep into the ground floor concourse through floor to ceiling glass. Canopies extend from inside the concourse to outside, amplifying the transparency and creating generous sheltered sidewalks.

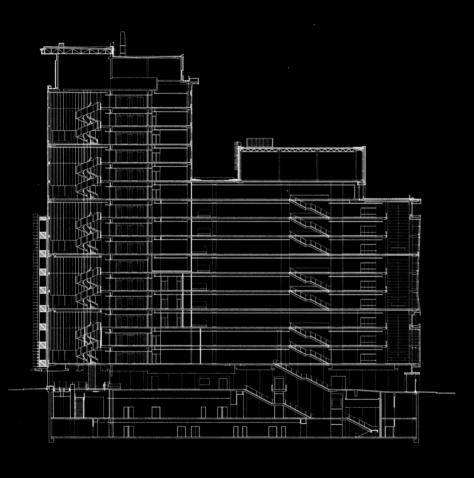

Kuwabara Payne McKenna Blumberg Architects
with Fichten Soiferman et Associés Architectes,
in joint venture
Toronto, Ontario and Montréal, Québec
www.kpmb.ca
www.fsa-arch.qc.ca

Bruce Kuwabara (KPMB)
b. 1949, Hamilton; B.Arch. (Toronto) 1972.
Marianne McKenna (KPMB)
b. 1950, Montréal; B.A. (Québec) 1972; M.Arch.
(Yale) 1976.
Andrew Dyke (KPMB)
b. 1966, Toronto; B.Arch. (Toronto) 1990.
Jacob Fichten (FSA)
b. 1941, Russia; B.Arch. (McGill) 1967.
Gerald Soiferman (FSA)
b. 1939, Montréal; B.Arch. (McGill) 1963.
Andrij Serbyn (FSA)
b. 1954, Montréal; B.F.A. (Concordia) 1976; B.Arch.
(Toronto) 1981.

Le Quartier Concordia, Concordia University
Montréal, Québec
Engineering/Computer Science & Visual Arts
Building 2000-2005
Competition Team
Bruce Kuwabara
Marianne McKenna
Andrew Dyke
Paulo Rocha
Julie Dionne
Catherine Venart
Project Team
Anne Marie Fleming
Glenn MacMullin
John Peterson
Bill Colaco
Michael Conway
Julie Dionne
Victor Garzon
Michael Hall
Eric Ho
Bernard Jacques
Rita Kiriakis
Dimitri Koubatis
Serge Labossière
Eugenio Laborde

Nicolas-Mallik Paquin
Angie Mende
Benoît Picard
André Préfontaine
Bertrand Marais
Meika McCunn
André Savoie
Lucy Timbers
André Tremblay
Deborah Wang
Chris Wegner
Ngae-Chi Wong
Xin Wu
Sandrine Zambou
Paolo Zasso
Structural Engineer
Nicolet Chartrand Knoll Limitée
Mechanical, Electrical & Sustainability Engineers
Pageau, Morel et associés, Dupras Ledoux ingénieurs
Keen Engineering
Cost Consultant
Curran McCabe Ravindran Ross Inc.
Code, Life Safety Consultant
Leber/Rubes Inc., Technorm Inc.
Furniture and Wayfinding
Moureaux Hauspy Design Inc.
Vertical Transportation
Exim
Audio-visual
Trizart-Alliance
Information Technology, Security
Doucet et Associés
General Contractor
Hervé Pomerleau Inc.
Public Art Installation
Nicolas Baier in conjunction with designers,
Bruno Braën and Hans Brown
Campus Master Plan
Groupe Cardinal Hardy Inc.
Project Manager
Genivar
3-D Model Rendering
Norm Li, KPMB
Q Studio
Model Fabrication
J.S. Models
Photography
Tom Arban

John Molson School of Business 2000-2007
Project Team
Robert Kastelic
John Peterson
Esther Cheung
Virginia Dos Reis
Omar Gandhi
Eric Ho
Eric Jofriet
Artur Kobylanski
Dimitri Koubatis
Martine Lacombe
Glenn MacMullin
Jill Osiowy
Lheila Palumbo
Olesia Stefurak
Lucy Timbers
Marie-Hélène Trudeau
Bertrand Marais
Structural Engineer
Nicolet Chartrand Knoll Limitée, Consultant S.M.
Mechanical & Electrical Engineer
Groupe HBA Experts-Conseils Senc.
Cost Consultant
Curran McCabe Ravindran Ross Inc.
Code, Life Safety Consultant
Technorm Inc.
Vertical Transportation
Exim
Audio-visual
Trizart Alliance
IT/Security
Doucet et Associés
Acoustics
Davidson Associates
Food Services
Bernard Associés
Campus Master Plan
Groupe Cardinal Hardy Inc.
Project Manager
Genivar
3-D Model Rendering
KPMB Architects
Models
L'Atelier Glaf
Photography
Tom Arban

BAIRD SAMPSON NEUERT
Erindale Hall,
University of Toronto, Mississauga

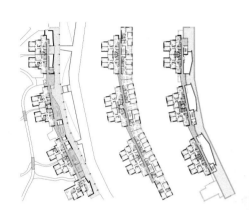

Erindale Hall embraces its spatial and temporal role as a place of transition for first year university students. Integrating built form with innate site attributes, this two hundred bed residence is designed to create a locus of collegial society that supports and enriches the quality of student experience. Opportunistically inserted into a "rift" in the forest, the building engages with this remnant of the Credit River Valley landscape to realize the founding generations' dream of a "northern campus."

The elongated plan of the building gives form to the "main street" of the campus. A "single-loaded" horizontal "bar" elevated over a colonnade provides cover for much of the central pedestrian route to the campus, known as the "five-minute walk." In contrast to the linear arrangement of four bedroom suites in the bar building, those on the west side of the building are clustered into vertical towers with gaps between them, revealing an internal corridor allowing daylight in and views to exterior landscapes.

The colonnade is designed to encourage social interaction and engage the landscape. Collective facilities are concentrated on the ground floor adjacent to the colonnade, behind a serpentine wall of alternating glass and massive limestone panels. Areas of transparency provide visual and physical linkages through the building. Contrasting with the reflected landscape of the smooth glass, massive fossilized stone panels recall the nearby Credit River's transit through time and space.

Bedrooms providing contemplative spaces aggregate with social space to support conviviality.

The horizontal bar is marked by individual punched windows offering each bedroom generous views of the "five minute walk" and the forest beyond, as well as daylighting and natural ventilation. Windows to living areas are grouped together to form super-scaled windows that are paired with glazed screens along the corridor side of each suite to create opportunities for views through the building. On the opposite side of the building, windows to living areas are grouped to form towers of glass that overlook open courtyards and the wetland forest. Most bedrooms have similar corner windows without mullions; each offering a closer, more individually engaged panoramic relationship to the landscape.

This project advances both micro and macro environmental objectives: the building is configured to preserve environmentally sensitive plant communities, and storm water is directed to the wetland forest as part of an ecological restoration strategy. The building integrates architectural and environmental control systems to reclaim heat and reduce overall energy consumption to 55 percent of the ASHRAE 90.1 energy allowance.

Baird Sampson Neuert Architects
Toronto, Ontario
www.bsnarchitects.com

George Baird
b. 1939, Toronto; B.Arch. (Toronto), 1962.
Barry Sampson
b. 1948, Oshawa; B.Arch. (Toronto), 1972.
Jon Neuert
b. 1962, Windsor; B.Arch. (Toronto), 1990.

Erindale Hall Student Residence,
University of Toronto
Mississauga, Ontario 2001-2003
Project Team
Colin Ripley
Ian Douglas
Structural Engineer
Yolles Partnership
Mechanical, Electrical Engineer
Crossey Engineering Ltd.
Site Services
EMC Group Limited
Landscape
Janet Rosenberg & Associates Landscape Architects Inc.
Sustainable Design
Ted Kesik
General Contractor
Ledcor Construction Limited
Photography
David Sisam
Michael Awad
Ian Douglas – BSN Architects

DIAMOND AND SCHMITT
Bahen Center
for Information Technology,
University of Toronto

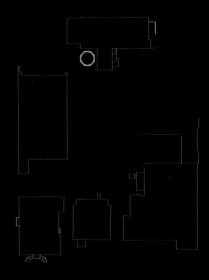

The Bahen Centre for Information Technology is designed to accommodate leading edge research and teaching in computer science and electrical engineering for the Faculty of Engineering and the Faculty of Arts and Science at the University of Toronto. The design of the Centre is intended to accommodate an academic community supported by technological innovation.

The building is shaped to exploit the many constraints of an eccentrically configured mid-block site, bordered by seven University buildings and a 32 metre height limit. The first three floors, occupied primarily by undergraduate programmes, are bisected by two arcades. A three-storey skylit arcade aligned east-west through the centre of the plan provides the principal point of access to lecture theatres, seminar rooms and computing labs. A north-south arcade opens to a south facing interior court and café. This axis extends south across a new outdoor quadrangle, along ramps, stairs and fountains and eventually establishes a new southern gateway into the University precinct. At the interior crossroads of these two axes, a vertical "landmark" stair rising through eight floors surrounds a glass tower of shared meeting rooms and lounges. The glass stair cylinder is skylit and forms a translucent lantern at night, drawing light deep into the centre of the building, forming a place of meeting and connection within the research community. The building is clad in pale ivory, hand-laid brick, with aluminum and frit glass sunshades.

The building uses an innovative under-floor servicing system for the distribution of all data, power, heating, ventilation and air-conditioning. This supports programme flexibility as well as displacement ventilation, resulting in a 50 percent improvement in air quality. Other sustainable design features include: a complete recovery of storm water for use in irrigation and other water-features; extensive solar shading to reduce the cooling plant; use of day-lighting seep into programme areas; use of recovery waster heat to provide 92 percent of the required heating load and an energy use of 53 percent of the new Model Energy Code of Canada.

Diamond and Schmitt Architects Inc.
Toronto, Ontario
www.dsai.ca

Donald Schmitt
b. 1951, South Porcupine, Ontario; B.Arch. (Toronto) 1978.
David Dow
b. 1961, Toronto; B.Arch. (Waterloo) 1988.
Thom Pratt
b. 1953, Ottawa; B.Arch. (Toronto) 1986.
Michael Leckman
b. 1957, Montréal; B.Arch. (Toronto) 1988.

Bahen Centre for Information Technology, University of Toronto
Toronto, Ontario 1999-2002
Project Team
Dale McDowell
Matthew Lella
Cecelia Chen
Sony Rai
Desmond Gregg
James Blendick
Terry Cecil
Leo Mieles
Dan Klinck
Edward Kim
Michael Gross
Agnes Kazmierczak
Dominique Morazain
Kirsten Douglas
Ian Douglas
Steve Bauer
Diana Saragosa
Frank Mazulla
Jennifer Trost
Natalie Drago
Structural Engineer
Read Jones Christofferson Ltd.
Mechanical Engineer
Keen Engineering
Electrical Engineer
Crossey Engineering Ltd.
Landscape
Diamond and Schmitt
Ian Grey & Associates
Cost Consultant
Curran McCabe Ravindran Ross Inc.
Code Consultant
Arencon Inc.
Audio-visual, Consultant
Imagineering Group Inc.
Photography
Steven Evans
Elizabeth Gyde

KOHN SHNIER
Umbra World Headquarters
Toronto

The renovation of a mundane industrial building located on a major highway in a bleak industrial landscape was a challenge to the designers. The goal was to create a fresh image that would represent the spirit of a youthful company within this inhospitable landscape. The client, a manufacturer of industrial designed products, required the project to be both timely and timeless; seemingly contradictory qualities, whilst creating an unmistakable identity. The solution, a sort of brise-soleil, acts like sunglasses; simultaneously masking and enhancing the subject.

Plastic was chosen as the major material. It relates to the client's product, and offers versatility in forming, colouring and detailing: it is light and proved quicker to install than glass (critical to cost and schedule), and it offers the possibility of mass production.

Four components were developed: a cantilevered screen mounted on the building; a free-standing screen addressing the entry; a sign/beacon identifying the building from the arterial road; and a roof-mounted, glass "lantern." The "lantern" creates a distinct architectural element that defers to the scale of the highway, while permitting diffuse light into the design department below it. At night, the glowing sign/scrim enhances the project's visibility.

The metre square, vacuum-formed panels are coloured to a translucency that capitalize on changing light effects, including artificial lighting at night. Slots cut into the panels allow the users an "edited view" of the surrounding landscape without feeling claustrophobic. A subtle glow radiates from the panels, creating soft light effects on the interior. Galvanized structural steel supports the panels that are attached to the frame using an adjustable steel fitting, which slides along a post-tensioned rod that also provides wind-load support.

Kohn Shnier Architects
Toronto, Ontario
www.kohnshnierarchitects.com

Martin Kohn
b. 1953, Toronto; B.ES., B.Arch. (Waterloo), 1978.
John Shnier
b. 1955, Toronto; B.ES., B.Arch. (Waterloo), 1979.

Umbra World Headquarters
Toronto, Ontario 1998-1999
Project Team
John Potter
Rick Galezowski
Structural Engineer
Blackwell Engineering Limited
Mechanical, Electrical Engineer
Enso Systems
Interior Design
Figure 3
Contractor
Urbacon Limited
Photography
Richard Seck
Richard Johnson
Kohn Shnier Architects

House in Erin Township

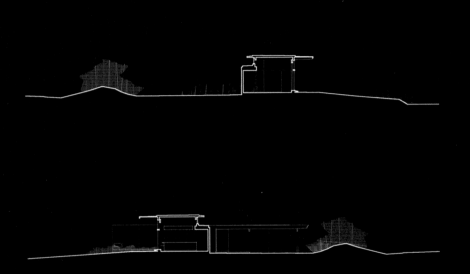

Competition Entry for
Canadian Ambassador's Residence, Berlin

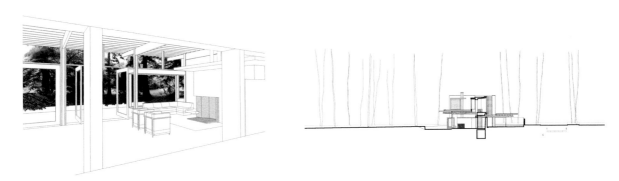

A constant within our work is the question of how to inhabit a site. Responding to the landscape "as found," how might we organize the way it can be experienced, mediating between the built and natural environment?

Three projects, Wychwood House, House in Erin Township, and the Competition Entry for a Residence for the Canadian Ambassador, Berlin, exemplify this method of working to expose the inherent qualities of a site. Each project draws on its surroundings, using sectional and planar relationships as unique readings into the character of the various landscapes. The result in each case is an experiential interaction between building and site. Whether in urban neighbourhoods (Wychwood House and the Residence for the Canadian Ambassador), or in a rural setting (House in Erin Township), the buildings all exemplify modest sitings, embedding themselves into their environments and creating a sense of retreat, while still making outward connections to the natural landscape. These projects express attitudes and ideas that are a focus in our work: developing legible, site specific architecture that articulates a clear design concept and strong sense of place.

Ian MacDonald Architect Inc.
Toronto, Ontario
www.ima.ca

Ian MacDonald
b. 1953, Kitchener, Ontario; B.ES. (Waterloo) 1975; B.Arch. (Carleton), 1978.

Wychwood House
Toronto, Ontario 2002-ongoing
Project Team
Olga Pushkar
Tim Wickens
Scott Sorli
Michael Attard
Structural Engineers
Blackwell Engineering Limited
Mechanical Engineers
Toews Systems Design
Millwork
Kobi's Cabinets
Contractor
Cened Construction
Stonemason
Gus Butterfield
Photography
Michael Awad

House in Erin Township
Ontario 2002
Project Team
Tim Wickens
Olga Pushkar
Michael Attard
Structural Engineer
Yolles Partnership Inc.
Mechanical Engineer
Toews Systems Design
Millwork
Gibson Greenwood Inc.
Contractor
Marcus Design Build
Photography
Tim Wickens
Ted Yarwood

Competition Entry for Residence for the Canadian Ambassador
Berlin 1997
Project Team
Kevin Weiss
Olga Pushkar
Scott Sorli
Model Fabrication
Ian Douglas
Arthur Billard
Watercolour
Guang Hao

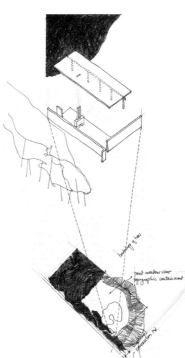

SHIM–SUTCLIFFE
Ledbury Park, Toronto

Ledbury Park began with the creation of a site. A new, artificially constructed topographic condition provides the context for this recreational facility and its surrounding landscape. The park's architectural and landscape features are integrated and interwoven throughout the project. Water weaves throughout the site, creating a physical link between a variety of programmatic elements.

The site was a level, three-acre park just north of Toronto, which occupies the leftover portions of a residential suburban block. The juxtaposition between the modest post-war bungalows and the newer maximum envelope stucco boxes illustrated the need for a new community centre and a new neighbourhood focus. The Parks and Recreation Department was an enlightened client, and from the outset they wanted to create a timeless project for the neighbourhood, while also addressing long-term maintenance and operational issues.

Ledbury Park consists of a sunken (300 feet long by 50 feet wide) pleasure skating canal, which

transforms into a shallow reflecting pool during the warmer months. The outdoor circular wading pool and swimming pool (75 feet long by 25 feet wide) are elevated three feet above grade to provide a vantage point for viewing the park. A linear brick change building links the skating rink and its adjacent year-round viewing pavilion with the swimming pool. A series of primary and secondary walkways, two pedestrian bridges and a plaza are used to connect the park to its surrounding neighbourhood. A large mechanical room occupies the lower level of the change building and contains both the filtration and refrigeration equipment.

Upon the existing terrain, a new artificial topography was constructed. The skating canal/reflecting pool is contained within an elongated rectangular plane set a few feet below grade; the excavated fill is used to form an earth berm, creating a grassy embankment. A Corten steel pedestrian bridge links both sides of the canal and provides elevated views of the rest of the park from the pool deck. A long brick building with its wooden trellis and

boardwalk houses swimming pool change rooms, and links the pool and the canal.

Brick garden walls, along with a dense row of pyramidal English oaks and custom designed lamp standards, line the main pedestrian route through the site. The elevated pedestrian walk that circumnavigates the skating canal/reflecting pool is defined on one side by a formal alleé of pleached lindens, and on the other two sides by a picturesque walk between sumacs, oaks and maples. The architectural promenade weaves together the custom Corten steel pedestrian bridge, wooden boardwalks, viewing pavilions, groves and alleés of trees, and an articulated public plaza.

The role of water in winter and summer was carefully orchestrated, providing changing dimensions to the project through each season. As a result, an architectural promenade was created by the connection of simple elements in a public landscape, resulting in a rich spatial experience for all viewers.

Shim-Sutcliffe Architects
Toronto, Ontario
www.shim-sutcliffe.com

Brigitte Shim
b. 1958, Kingston, Jamaica; B.ES. (Waterloo), 1981;
B.Arch. (Waterloo), 1983.
Howard Sutcliffe
b. 1958, Yorkshire, England; B.ES. (Waterloo), 1981;
B.Arch. (Waterloo), 1983.

Ledbury Park
Toronto, Ontario 1996-1997
Architect of Record
G+G Partnership Architects
Structural Engineer
Baerjee Anderson & Associates Inc.
Mechanical, Electrical Engineer
Rybka, Smith and Ginsler Ltd.
Landscape
NAK Design Group

Consultants
Dan Euser, Water Architecture
R.J. Van Seters Co. Ltd.
Eagle Bridge
Margaret Priest
Lumca
Tremonte Manufacturing Limited
Builder
Carosi Construction
Upton Durish
Model Fabrication
Richard Sinclair with Steven Fox and John Featherstone
Client
City of North York, Parks & Recreation Department
Model Photography
Steven Evans
Michael Awad
Photography
James Dow
Presentation Drawings
Donald Chong

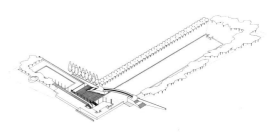

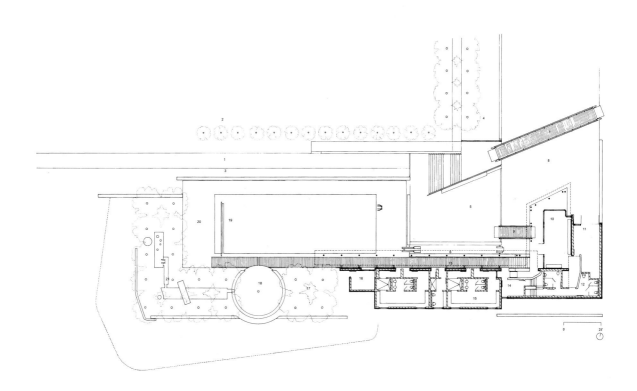

SAUCIER + PERROTTE
Perimeter Institute for Theoretical Physics, Waterloo

Riding the controversial line between public and private space, this private research institute attempts to subvert the usual hard thresholds established by private enterprise in the public realm. The site is on the shore of Silver Lake, at the northern edge of Waterloo's downtown core and the southern edge of the city's central park. Adjacent to the primary pedestrian access between the university campus and the city centre, the site is an urban wilderness between clearly defined worlds.

The design is also inspired by the nebulous spaces occupied by the subjects of theoretical physics, at once micro- and macro-cosmic, rich in information and of indeterminate form and substance. Between city and park, the Perimeter Institute expands and inhabits the improbable space of the line that separates the two. The building defines the secure zones of the Institute's facilities within a series of parallel glass walls, embedded in an erupting ground plane that reveals a large reflecting pool. The north façade, facing the park across this pool, reveals the Institute as an organism; a microcosm of discrete elements. The south façade, facing the city across train tracks and the city's main arterial road, presents the Institute as a unified but transforming entity of enigmatic scale and content. Entry into the Institute is possible from both the north, along the reflecting pool, and south, under the new ground.

The interior of the Institute is organized around two central spaces; the main hall on the ground floor and the garden on the first level. Spaces for administration, meeting and seminar rooms, leisure and fitness spaces, and a multi-purpose theatre for symposia and public presentations, have direct access to the main hall. The circulation corridors running east-west are sandwiched between the opalescent glass planes, which are occasionally punctured or shifted to reveal views across the interior space of the hall. Vertical circulation climbs these walls, tendrils of ground that run from the garden through the building. The garden—nature emerging from the vacuum— is crossed by three bridges that puncture all the planes, as well as the north and south façades. The bridges are conduits for quick access to facilities, information and colleagues; routes crossing the improbable space between theoretical physics and everyday life.

Saucier + Perrotte architectes
Montréal, Québec
www.saucierperrotte.com

Gilles Saucier
b. 1958, Sainte-Francoise, Québec; B.Arch. (Laval), 1982.
André Perrotte
b. 1959, Sainte-Foy, Québec; B.Arch. (Laval), 1982.

Perimeter Institute for Theoretical Physics
Waterloo, Ontario 2001-2004
Project Team
Trevor Davies
Andrew Butler
Dominique Dumais
Eric Majer
Pierre-Alexandre Rhéaume
Anna Bendix
Sudhir Suri
Christian Hébert
Laurence LeBeux

Quinlan Osborne
Jean-Louis Léger
Samantha Schneider
Nathalie Cloutier
Christine Levine
Jean-François Lagacé
Sergio Morales
Guillaume Sasseville
Maxime Gagné
Audrey Archambault
Structural Engineer
Blackwell Engineering Limited
Mechanical, Electrical Engineer
Crossey Engineering Ltd.
Civil Engineering
Stantec Consulting Ltd.
Acoustics
Acoustics Engineering Ltd.
Audio-visual
Novita

Kitchens
YGQ Designer Inc.
Landscape Architect
Saucier + Perrotte architectes
Contractor
Eastern Construction Company Limited
Client
Perimeter Institute
Photography
Marc Cramer
Saucier + Perrotte architectes

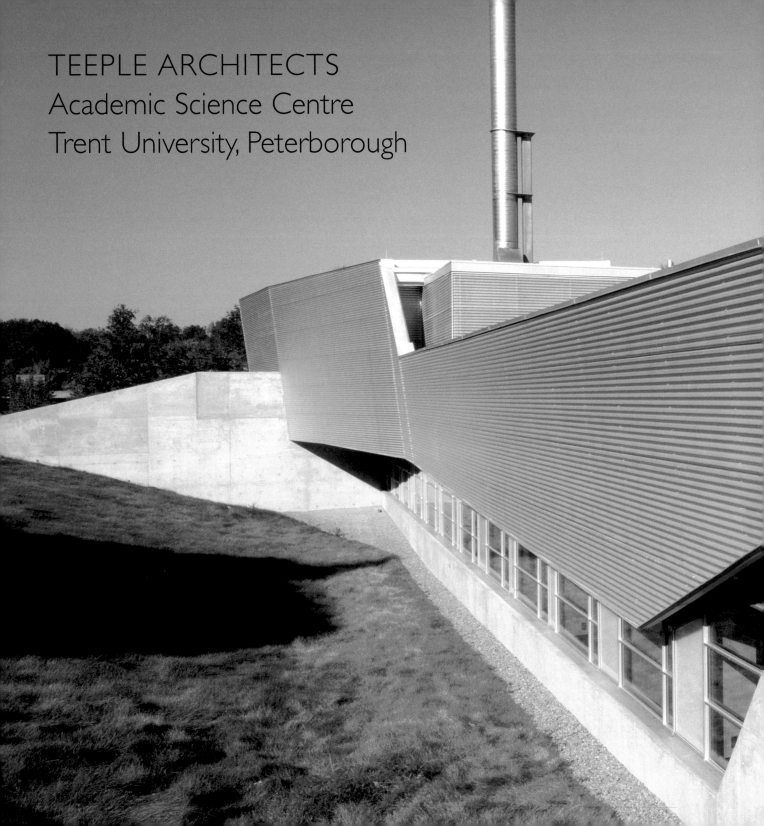

TEEPLE ARCHITECTS
Academic Science Centre
Trent University, Peterborough

Early Learning Centre
University of Toronto, Toronto

These two projects, designed simultaneously in 2001, seek to evolve spatial concepts particular to the special nature of their users, and in tune with the very different character of their settings.

The Academic Science Centre at Trent University is set into the beautiful landscape of the banks of the Ottanabee River near Peterborough, Ontario. The building is conceived as an extension of this landscape; its living roofs extend out from the banks and link to the "+15" pedestrian system that connects the campus. In so doing, three new courtyards are created on the campus. A narrative walk weaves through this landscape, interconnecting existing buildings to one another and to the river. This walk descends through the roof garden to the river, presenting views of Trent's beautiful landscape to students as they move through the campus and the new building. The river is the constant reference point of the design; it is continuously present in one's experience of the place.

Two flexible and rationally ordered wings of research space are linked to a third wing of teaching labs at a casual meeting space. This "joint" looks back into a court cut into the river bank and outward to the river. The ordered nature of the work spaces contrasts with the sculpted complexity of the public space as it reaches outward from the river bank.

The Early Learning Centre at the University of Toronto, set in the heart of the city, creates a multi-dimensional landscape of play in an urban context. Overlapping folds in the building's surface define a wide range of spatial conditions, including lofts from which to survey each playroom, and small protected spaces that offer views to infant playrooms on the lower level, where recessed pits define focal points of play. Every surface of the centre's compact site is devoted to the learning experience of children, including the ramp that links each of the two principal playroom floors, and the roofs of the building that form outdoor play spaces on multiple levels. The architecture is intended to embody an enriched range of spatial experiences that spark the imagination, encourage multiple readings, and present an extended range of play opportunities for the building's young inhabitants.

Teeple Architects Inc.
Toronto, Ontario
www.teeplearch.com

Stephen R. Teeple
b. 1954, St. Thomas, Ontario; B.ES., B.Arch. (Waterloo), 1977, 1980;
M.Sc.B.D. (Columbia) 1989.

Academic Science Centre, Trent University
Peterborough, Ontario 2001-2004
with Shore Tilbe Irwin & Partners in joint venture
Project Team
Chris Radigan
Matthew Smith
Myles Craig
Mark Baechler
Dean Lavigne
Anya Moryoussef
Stephen Irwin
Steven Ploeger
Jan Willem Gritters
Terry Leventos
Bob Ashby
Structural Engineer
Yolles Partnership Inc.
Mechanical Engineer
Smith and Andersen Consulting Engineering
Electrical Engineer
Crossey Engineering Ltd.
Landscape
The MBTW Group
Photography
Tom Arban

Early Learning Centre, University of Toronto
Toronto, Ontario 2001-2003
Project Team
Cheryl Atkinson
Bernard Jin
Tom Arban
Dean Lavigne
Structural Engineer
Yolles Partnership Inc.
Mechanical Engineer
Keen Engineering
Electrical Engineer
Crossey Engineering Ltd.
Landscape Consultant
The MBTW Group
Photography
Tom Arban

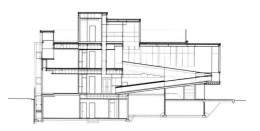

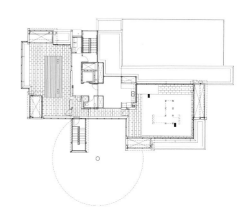

architectsALLIANCE
High-rise Housing in Toronto

MoZo

District Lofts

Woodsworth Colledge Student Residence
University of Toronto

Pond Road Student Residence
York University

Spire

TipTop Lofts

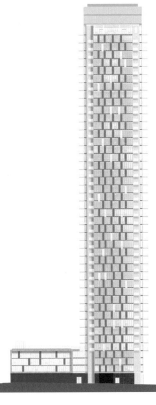

Housing makes cities. Theory's rediscovery of the city, and its reification of urbanism over the past three decades, has been inversely proportional to practice's involvement in mass housing. While residential construction constitutes over 80 percent of building activity in North America, this activity occurs beyond the purview of the salon.

The housing problem was once a fundamental project of the Modern Movement. Reeling from the failures of post-war urban renewal initiatives, and recently discredited as a valid policy issue by neo-liberalism, housing has been left to the vagaries of the market place. The hegemony of the development industry and the commodification of dwelling have silenced design culture. At the present moment, housing has lost its architectural cachet.

Yet housing is central to our practice. We believe that residential architecture is a rich and challenging field of endeavour. The projects illustrated include two student residences and four market condominiums. The student residences have different unit types, different contexts, and different pedagogical agendas. The Pond Road Student Residence at York University is Canada's first sustainable student residence. The four condominiums, built for one developer client, were each generated by very different and very specific approaches to unit design.

Each of these projects address a series of similar architectural issues—the reinterpretation of dwelling unit, the provision of amenity, the development of a fabric building vocabulary that is

both compelling and appropriate, the articulation of a convincing and urbane response to density, and the enrichment of the public realm. Each of these projects is a very conscious act of city building.

We embrace the messiness and vitality of the contemporary city, and are willing to navigate the complexities, challenges and compromises necessary for its construction. We enjoy the scale, ambition and essential optimism of developers. In no small part, the general awfulness of our cities is due to the studied refusal of committed architects to involve themselves in their dreams. The present situation is not perfect, but it is all we have. We believe our efforts and our involvement can make it better.

architectsAlliance
Toronto, Ontario
www.architectsalliance.com

Ralph Bergman
b. 1942, Montréal; B.Arch. (McGill), 1967;
M.Arch. (UC Berkeley), 1970.
Peter Clewes
b. 1955, Victoria; B.ES. (Waterloo), 1976;
B.Arch. (Waterloo), 1979.
Adrian Di Castri
b. 1952, Victoria; B.Arch. (Toronto), 1982.
Patricia Hanson
b. 1955, Regina; B.F.A. (Manitoba), 1977;
M.Arch. (Manitoba), 1981.
John van Nostrand
b. 1949, Toronto; B.Arch. (Toronto), 1972.
Rudy Wallman
b. 1954, Windsor; B.ES. (Waterloo), 1976;
B.Arch. (Waterloo), 1979.

MoZo 2000-2003
District Lofts 1999-2001
TipTop Tailors Building Residential Conversion 2001-2004
Spire 2002-2005
Pond Road Student Residence, York University 2001-2004
Woodsworth College Student Residence,
University of Toronto 2000-2003

Project Team
Walter Bettio
Pui-to Chau
Adam Feldmann
Prishram Jain
Jan Adegeest
David J. Agro
Fred Allin

Martin Inglis Baron
Rogelio Bayaton
Emily Best
Graeme Burt
Rob Cadeau
Winston Chong
Joginder Dhanjal
Deni Di Filippo
Bruce Fraser
Joshua Frederic
Heather Gallagher
Behna Ghanizadeh-Namini
Janis Hamacher
Nicole Hamilton
Takuma Handa
Pia Heine
Sanja Janjanin
Monika Jaroszonek
Cassie Kent
Akshay Kumar J. Joshi
Al Kably
Emerich Kaspar
Paul Kulig
Stan Leonowicz
Nathan Marentette
Mary K. McIntyre
Joseph Moro
Dieter Neitsch
Mara Nicolaou
Fatema Panju
Deni Papetti
Jason Petrunia
Bahram Pezeshki
Anthony Provenzano
Blair Robinson
Heather Rolleston
Marcella Romita

John Sadar
David Steiner
Kevin Steltzer
Jon van Oostveen
Peter van Rooy
Marcia Walker
Stephen Wells
Elcin Yeter
Barbara Zee
Structural Engineer
Halsall Associates Limited
Jablonsky, Ast and Partners
Read Jones Christoffersen Ltd.
Yolles Group Inc.
Mechanical, Electrical Engineer
CBM Group Ltd.
Hidi Rae Consulting Engineers Inc.
Lam & Associates
MCW Consultants Ltd.
Landscape
Corban and Goode Landscape Architecture and Urbanism
Diana Gerrard Landscape Architecture
Ferris + Associates Inc.
Conservation Architect
E.R.A. Architects Inc.
Clients
Context Development
University of Toronto
York University
Photography
Tom Arban
Winston Chong
Lenscape
Gareth Long
Ben Rahn

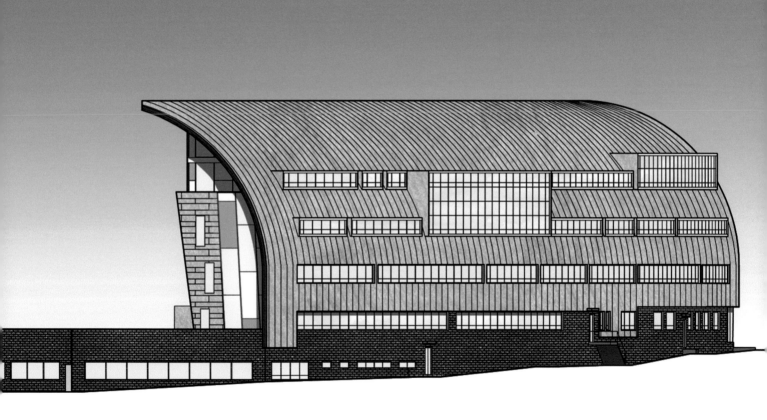

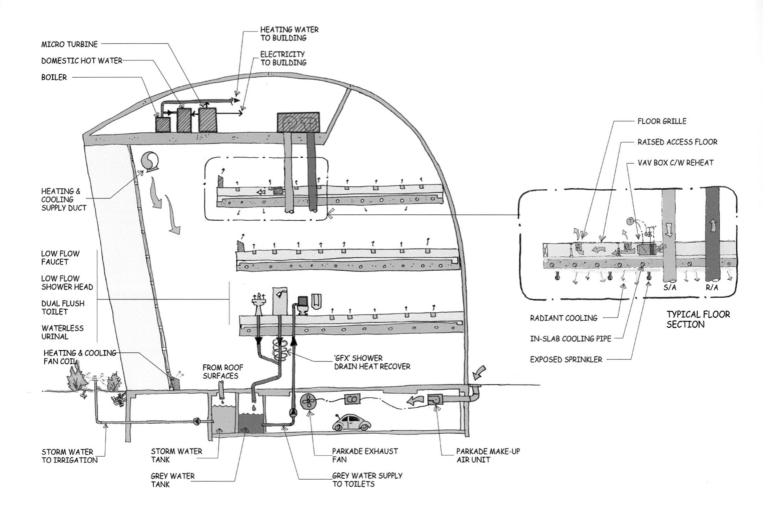

MICRO TURBINE
DOMESTIC HOT WATER
BOILER
HEATING WATER TO BUILDING
ELECTRICITY TO BUILDING
HEATING & COOLING SUPPLY DUCT
LOW FLOW FAUCET
LOW FLOW SHOWER HEAD
DUAL FLUSH TOILET
WATERLESS URINAL
HEATING & COOLING FAN COIL
FROM ROOF SURFACES
'GFX' SHOWER DRAIN HEAT RECOVER
STORM WATER TO IRRIGATION
STORM WATER TANK
GREY WATER TANK
PARKADE EXHAUST FAN
GREY WATER SUPPLY TO TOILETS
PARKADE MAKE-UP AIR UNIT

FLOOR GRILLE
RAISED ACCESS FLOOR
VAV BOX C/W REHEAT
RADIANT COOLING
IN-SLAB COOLING PIPE
EXPOSED SPRINKLER
S/A   R/A

TYPICAL FLOOR SECTION

In the first phase of redevelopment of an industrial site into a civic office precinct, the new Municipal Water Treatment Centre in Calgary meshes two City departments: Waterworks and Waste Water. The building is expressive of the water-based nature of the programme and clad in galvanized aluminum and glazed with a high efficiency curtain wall system, and appropriate to LEED standards. Calgary is the first Canadian city to mandate that all their new buildings meet a minimum LEED Silver standard.

The site lies on the north edge of the brownfield redevelopment. The curve of its boundary, a major roadway, is the remnant of an historic railroad.

The narrow footprint abuts the north boundary, so that the building acts as a garden wall and renders the south portion of the site as garden. The building section offers energy efficiency, as well as sheltering frontage to the roadway and protection to the garden. Open offices line the north perimeter, with double height studio windows facing north to the city skyline. The offices enjoy views to the south and north. Solar impact is reduced due to large roof overhangs, patterns of glazing density and placement of meeting rooms. Circulation runs along the south face; a four-storey space that connects the previously distinct departments through the linear stair.

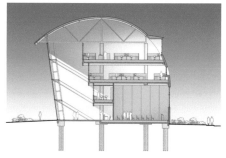

Sturgess Architecture
with Manasc Isaac Architects in joint venture
Calgary, Alberta
www.sturgessarchitecture.com

Jeremy Sturgess
b. 1949, Montréal; B.Arch. (Toronto), 1974.

Municipal Water Treatment Centre
Calgary, Alberta 2004-ongoing
Project Team
Lesley A. Beale
Courtney Clarke
Kirsten Dow Pierce
Vance Harris
Bob Horvath
Thomas Leong
Vivian Manasc

Keith Annett
Don Becker
Derek Heslop
Jonah Humphrey
John Murphy
Shauna Noyes
Kelly Sawatzky
Wes Sims
Steve Vallerand
Structural Engineer
Read Jones Christoffersen Ltd.
Mechanical, Electrical Engineer
Keen Engineering
Civil Engineering
Urban Systems
Landscape
Carlyle + Associates

MARC BOUTIN
Ramsay "Social Condensers," Calgary

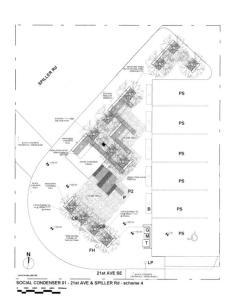

SOCIAL CONDENSER 01 - 21st AVE & SPILLER Rd - scheme 4

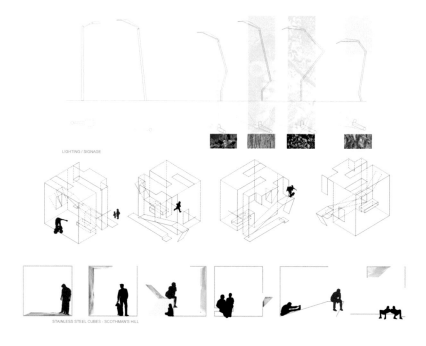

LIGHTING / SIGNAGE

STAINLESS STEEL CUBES - SCOTHMAN'S HILL

URBAN ARMATURE

CONCRETE / WOOD BENCH TRANSFORMATION

CONCRETE WALL / PAVING / BENCH TRANSFORMATION

WOOD BENCH / SURFACE TRANSFORMATION

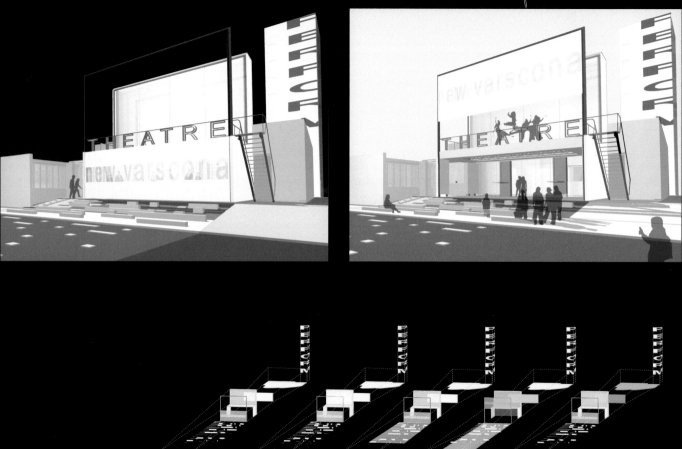

PUBLIC INFRASTRUCTURE   BUILDING AS A MARQUEE   BUILDING AS PUBLIC SPACE   BUILDING AS PUBLIC EVENT   BUILDING AS THEATRE

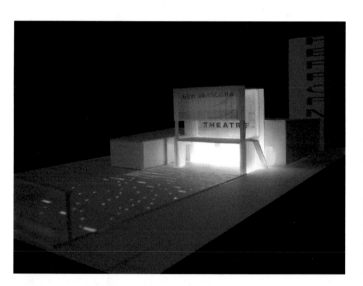

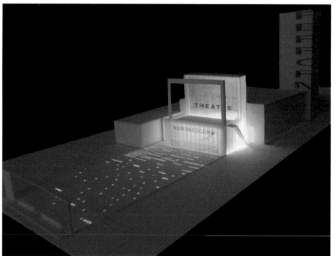

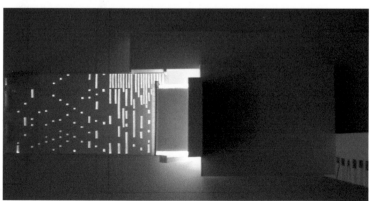

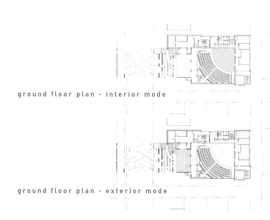

ground floor plan - interior mode

ground floor plan - exterior mode

The Agency Group Studios
Calgary

"Negotiable space" is a concept that seeks to socially activate the public realm, and space in general, through the transformation of passive users into active participants. "Negotiable space" is defined through two ideas. The first idea is the reconceptualizaton of mono-functional and hierarchical space into an open-ended, non-prescriptive spatial matrix. To this end, finite delineations of space, including conventional dichotomies such as interior/exterior, private/public, and served/service, are erased in favour of more fluid and inclusive relationships between spaces, functions and people. The second idea is the provision of anticipatory infrastructure as the primary spatial framework. In its expanded definition, anticipatory infrastructure provides the services that activate the spatial transformations necessary for different conditions of appropriation. Together, these concepts present space and the public realm as an incomplete project, to be engaged, reclaimed and constructed by its users.

At the root of "negotiable space" is a deep suspicion of formal mechanisms that advocate a finite definition of public space concretized in a specific form. Instead, "negotiable space" presents the public realm as a verb, or process, and therefore in a continuous state of evolution.

The Ramsay Redevelopment Plan is an on-going, comprehensive study that includes urban design, planning, landscape design, architectural design and lighting design. The study identified a number of external pressures on this inner city neighbourhood and developed three concepts in response. "Green Fingers" developed a reconnection of the community through the extensions of the green parkway along the Elbow River to the west. "Syncopation" created a pedestrian infrastructure that added strategic friction along the vehicular routes through the community to calm traffic. Finally, "Densification" developed rezoning strategies to redefine eroding edges of the community due to industrial expansion along its borders. Six specific architectural and urban interventions titled, "Social Condensers," and based on a language of standardized and transformable elements were designed to activate the public realm at sites seen as pregnant urban conditions.

The addition and renovation to the New Varscona Theatre in Edmonton, the busiest experimental theatre in Canada, is focused on the "front-of-house." To accommodate this programme, a one-storey pavilion is extruded from the existing openings that were the vehicle entry of the converted fire station. The pavilion gains its conceptual value by functioning as a cultural infrastructure: "building as marquee" and "building as stage."

In "building as marquee," the design's translucent skin, developed from research in insulated fibreglass technology, glazed light scoop, and painted hose drying tower, provide signage that acts as an urban lantern for both the theatre and the entire cultural district of Strathcona. In "building as public stage," the façade of the pavilion is counterbalanced so as to be able to be raised above the roof. In this position, it forms part of an infrastructural "proscenium arch" that supports the use of the pavilion roof as a stage for the outdoor festivals that take place in this area. In this arrangement, the roof and foyer act as a two-storey stage for outdoor performances, while the street is activated as audience space. A landscape of concrete benches, lit from underneath, can be occupied informally or as performance seating.

The Agency Group Studios in Calgary is an interior design to accommodate a collaborative work environment featuring different creative and production groups. The design was conceived as an interactive staging ground for collaborations of all types and is based on two ideas. First, the work areas are defined by an undulating amenity wall, or "performative surface," within which all building services, from conditioned air to data cabling, are contained. This "performative surface" conditions all spaces that are appropriated and used in an infinite number of ways. Next, the interior spaces have flexible/operable surfaces: for example, sliding glass partitions and chalkboard charette walls that allow them to connect with other spaces and be transformed to adapt to different work situations. The spectrum of complete privacy to public space is easily negotiated.

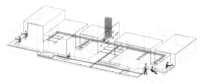

Marc Boutin Architect
Calgary, Alberta
www.mb-architect.ca

Marc Boutin
b. 1964, Aylmer, Québec; B.ES. (Manitoba) 1985;
B.Arch. (UBC) 1990; M.A. Arch. His. (Calgary) 2000.

Ramsay "Social Condensers"
Calgary, Alberta 2002-2005
Project Team
Mauricio Rosa
Matthew Stanley
George Mitch
Photography
Marc Boutin Architect

The Agency Group Studios
Calgary, Alberta 2004-ongoing
Project Team
Matthew Stanley
Mauricio Rosa
Photography
Marc Boutin Architect

New Varscona Theatre
Edmonton, Alberta 2003-ongoing
Project Team
Mauricio Rosa
Tony Leong
Matthew Stanley
Structural Engineer
Read Jones Christoffersen Ltd.
Mechanical Engineer
Keen Engineering
Electrical Engineer
Strebnicki Robertson & Associates
Landscape
Archifolia
Quantity Surveyors
BTY Group
Photography
Marc Boutin Architect

PATKAU ARCHITECTS
Strawberry Vale
Elementary School, Victoria

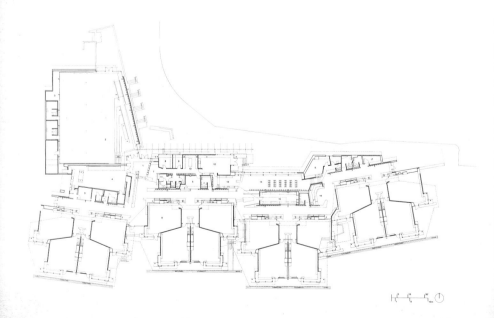

Strawberry Vale is a public school containing sixteen classrooms and support areas for students from kindergarten to grade seven. All classrooms are oriented toward the south to optimize natural light and to maximize the connection to the adjacent Garry Oak woodland. The classrooms are located on-grade, grouped in pods of four, providing direct access to the outdoors and the possibility of an extended programme of teaching. This arrangement of classroom pods creates a series of in-between spaces, both interior and exterior, suitable for individuals or small groups.

A meandering circulation spine provides access to each classroom pod and to the remaining components of the programme. The irregular configuration of the spine creates small-scale common spaces that support a variety of activities and interactions, both spontaneous and planned, providing an architectural basis for a greater sense of community within the school.

The school was developed within the context of environmental sustainability. Heating and lighting systems were designed to optimize the use of solar energy and daylight, while materials were selected to maximize environmental quality and minimize the amount of embodied energy. The hydrology of the site was carefully developed, integrating building systems with natural ones.

Patkau Architects Inc.
Vancouver, British Columbia
www.patkau.ca

John Patkau
b. 1947, Winnipeg; B.ES. (Manitoba), 1969; M.Arch. (Manitoba), 1972.
Patricia Patkau
b. 1950, Winnipeg; B.ID. (Manitoba), 1973; M.Arch. (Yale), 1978.
Michael Cunningham
b. 1955, Calgary; M.Env.Des. (Architecture) (Calgary), 1982.

Strawberry Vale Elementary School
Victoria, British Columbia 1992-1996
Project Team
Grace Cheung
Michael Kothke
Tim Newton
David Shone
Peter Suter
Jacqueline Wang
Structural Engineer
C.Y. Loh Associates Ltd.
Mechanical Engineer
DW Thomson Consultants Ltd.
Electrical Engineer
Reid Crowther & Partners Ltd.
Landscape
Moura Quayle/Lanark Consultants
Fire Protection
Gage-Babcock & Associates
Costing
BTY Group
Acoustics
Barron Kennedy Lyzun & Associates Ltd.
Photography
James Dow

JAMES K.M. CHENG
High-rise Housing in Vancouver

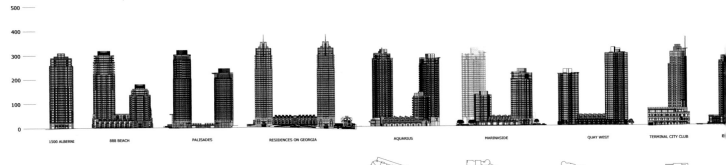

600

500

400

300

200

100

0

1500 ALBERNI · 888 BEACH · PALISADES · RESIDENCES ON GEORGIA · AQUARIUS · MARINASIDE · QUAY WEST · TERMINAL CITY CLUB

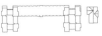

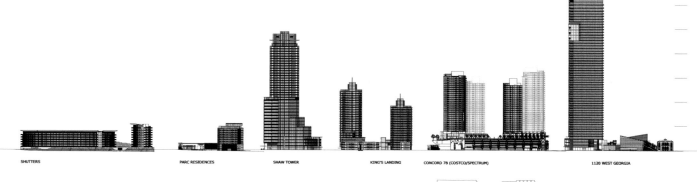

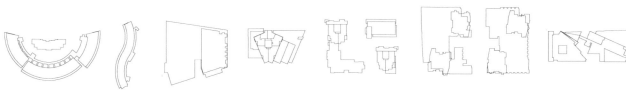

SHUTTERS   PARC RESIDENCES   SHAW TOWER   KING'S LANDING   CONCORD 7B (COSTCO/SPECTRUM)   1120 WEST GEORGIA

The work of James K.M. Cheng Architects Inc. is primarily focused on high density urban residential and mixed-use projects, ranging from stand-alone buildings to the planning of urban neighbourhoods. The firm believes buildings are part of the city fabric; there to define public and private spaces. The spaces between buildings are more important than the individual buildings and the landscape and interior realms are inextricable extensions of the project.

All of the firm's major projects include "secret gardens" with lush planting and water features. These secluded gardens are designed as urban oases, providing areas of calm in the epicentre of urban activity. They are designed both as social and visual counterpoints to the buildings; it is in these gardens that social interactions take place.

Orientation to view and light are the primary objectives of residential unit layouts in Vancouver, resulting in transparent buildings with open-plan interiors. Tall, slim towers combined with ground-oriented town houses have become the norm for high density residential developments in Vancouver. The town houses provide a human scale and "eyes on the street" for security. This typology is now often referred to as the "Vancouver Style" in the city planning and developer communities.

Previously, most of the firm's work has been in Vancouver. Currently, the firm is developing these approaches through projects in different cultural and geographical regions as diverse as Beijing,

Dallas, San Diego, Hawaii, Edmonton and Montréal. Such opportunities allow the firm to learn how working in different regions influences the design of the eventual urban form.

James K.M. Cheng Architects Inc.
Vancouver, British Columbia
info@jamescheng.com

James Cheng
b. 1947, Hong Kong; B.Arch. (Washington) 1970; M.Arch. (Harvard) 1977.

888 Beach Avenue 1993
Project Architect
Terrence Mott

Palisades 1996
Project Architect
Terrence Mott

Residences on Georgia 1998
Project Architect
Terrence Mott

Terminal City Club 1998
with Musson Cattell Mackey Partnership in joint venture
Project Architect
Gerry Ruehle

Quayside Marina 2002
Project Architect
Jones Lee

Escala 2002
Project Architect
Jones Lee

Shaw Tower 2005
Project Architect
Dawn Guspie/Norman Huth

Living Shangri-La 2005-ongoing
Project Architect
Dawn Guspie/Norman Huth

Urban Fare Architect
The Abbarch Partnership Architects
Structural Engineers
Glotman Simpson
Jones Kwong Kishi Consulting Engineers
Mechanical Engineers
Yoneda & Associates
Keen Engineering
Sterling, Cooper & Associates Ltd.
VEL Engineering
Electrical Engineers
Nemetz (S/A) & Associates Ltd.
Falcon Engineering Ltd.
Sokulski Engineering Ltd.
Geotechnical/Shoring Engineers
Terra MacLeod Geotechnical Ltd.
Geopacific Consultants Ltd.
MacLeod Geotechnical Ltd.
Cook Pickering & Doyle Ltd.
Project Manager (Terminal City)
NW Fletcher & Associates Ltd.
Contractors
Ledcor Construction Ltd.
PCL Constructors Canada Inc.
Scott Management Ltd.
Centreville Construction Ltd.
Elevator Consultant
John W. Gunn Consultants Inc.
Acoustics
Brown Strachan Associates
LEED Accredited Professional
Keen Engineering
Public Art Consultant
Lynne Diana Werker
Landscape
Phillips Farevaag Smallenberg Inc.
Sharp & Diamond Landscape Architecture
Christopher Phillips & Associates Ltd.
Surveyors
Ken K. Wong & Associates

Butler, Sundvick & Associates
Barnett Treharne Yates
Underhill Geomatics Ltd.
Matson Peck and Topliss
Papove Professional Land Surveying Inc.
Civil Engineer
Bovar-Concord Environmental
Soil Consultants
Norecol Environmental Consultant
MacLeod Geotechnical Ltd.
Curtain Wall Consultants
Brook Van Dalen & Associates Limited
Morrison Hershfield Group Inc.
Residential Technology Consultant
Millson Multi-Media Inc.
Code Consultants
Locke MacKinnon Domingo Gibson & Associates Ltd.
Gage-Babcock & Associates Ltd.
Interior Design
Robert M. Ledingham Inc.
Mitchell Freedland Design
MCM Interiors Ltd.
Fraser Design
Traffic Consultant
Ward Consultants Group
Specification Writer
J. Findlay & Associates Ltd.
Graphic Designer
Zacharko Design Partnership
Building Envelope Consultants
Building Performance Analysts Ltd.
RDH Building Engineering Ltd.
Technology Consultant
Millson Multi-Media Inc.
Marketing Consultant
Rennie Marketing Systems
Security Consultants
John Gunn W. Consultants Inc.
Intercon Security

Cost Consultants
Norson Construction Ltd.
Hanscomb Consultants Inc.
Renderings
Robert McIllhargey
Model Fabrication
A&B Scale Model
Clients
Hillsboro Investment Inc.
Concord Pacific
Shaw Communications/Westbank Projects Corp.
Park Georgia Development Ltd.
Pacific Palisades Hotel Ltd./Westbank Projects Corp.
Westbank Projects Corp./Ledcor Properties/
Peterson Investment Group Inc.
Terminal City Project Ltd. Partnership
Photography
James K.M. Cheng
Peter Aaron
Roger Brooks
Nic Lehoux

Shop Lift: Rethinking Retail
Richmond

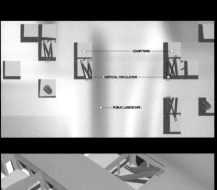

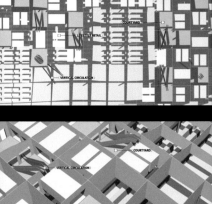

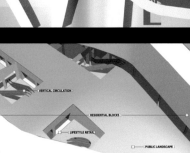

At once a shopping, residential and recreational complex, Shop Lift: Rethinking Retail envisions a hybrid consumer environment that is strategically integrated with open public spaces and private dwelling units. The resulting architectural typology is analogous, in formal and operational terms, to the term "plex," which means "to plait (interlace), or to interweave," thus forming a plexus: a complex body, collection, or set of things; a web, network or any very intertwined or interwoven mass. As with a human or animal structure consisting of closely bundled and intercommunicating tubes, nerves and vessels, the model presented here compresses a number of known and distinct programmes into a dense and highly functioning system. At opportune moments, this combinative strategy relies on the doubling up of, or mutation of necessary elements. The continuous column grid equally accommodates the spatial demands and circulation logics of a multi-level parking structure or shed-like, big-box outlet at the base. It supports a deep waffle structure knotted with smaller boutiques, which are experienced in sections from below and above. Above, this thick layer becomes a giant carpet, with the weft and warp of the structure modulating to allow a new topography to unroll across the site. This landscape is programmed with public amenities and is perforated with voids and courtyards to allow for vertical access and light to penetrate below. Residential units organized in floating bars constitute the final layer in the integrated system.

The integrated nature of Shop Lift proposes a maximization of land use and an economy of building stemming from shared infrastructures and structural components. The combination of programmes act to fuse the urban with the suburban; at once affording the convenience of large payload, big-box shopping, the lure of more specialized and intimate boutiques found on downtown streets and in shopping malls, and the benefits of living and playing within close proximity to both. As in a human plexus, the proximal systems can, and often have to work independently. Just as shopping and habitation remain distinct activities (inasmuch as lifestyle is not life), Shop Lift is an integrated scheme that is careful not to compromise the essential function of each incorporated programme. It respects the conventions and limitations of the various programmes in terms of access, privacy and economic viability, while enhancing the social and experiential possibilities afforded by this newly bundled system.

Shop Lift is a versatile prototype that seeks to expand previous notions of what a "shopping centre" can and could be. Here it is shown inserted into the centre of Richmond, BC— a suburb renowned for its innovative shopping mall developments, many influenced by Asian consumer culture.

George Yu Architects Inc.
Los Angeles, California
www.georgeyuarchitects.com

George Yu
b. 1964, Hong Kong; B.A. (UBC), 1985; M.Arch. (UCLA), 1988.

Shop Lift: Rethinking Retail
Richmond, BC 2004
Project Team
Konstantinos Chrysos
Marianthi Tatari
Research & Communications
Linda Hart
Installation Team
Owen Gerst
Yosuke Sugiyama
Model Fabrication
Carole Yu
Economic Analysis
David Bergman, Economics Research Associates
"Shop Lift" text
An Te Liu

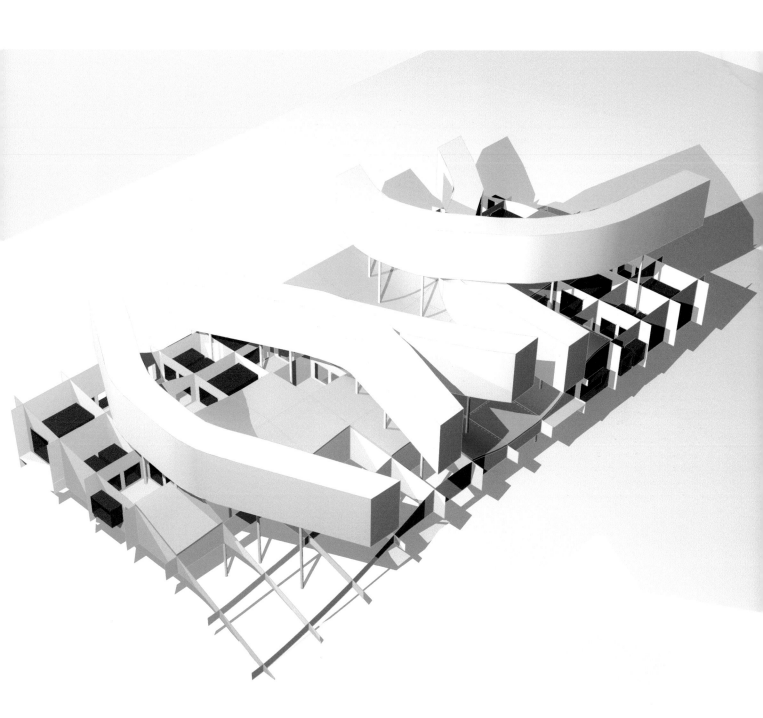

Appleton Residence, Saanich

Duplex, Vancouver

Fourplex, Vancouver

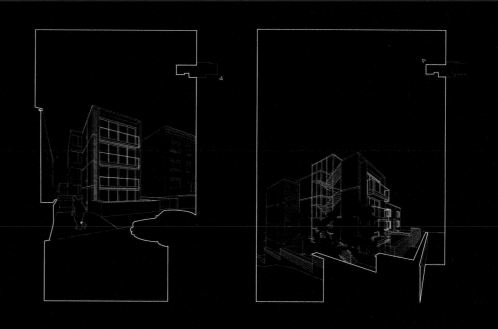

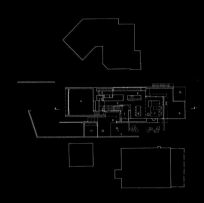

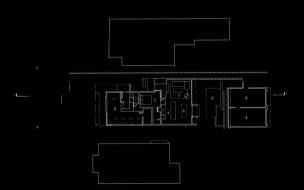

As an emerging practice, BattersbyHowat pursues an architectural expression that is modest and without pretense. The work explores the convergence of pragmatic and poetic concerns. The three projects represented here share particular affinities; each project explores and expresses the potential of developing and defining reciprocal relationships between landscape and artifice.

The Appleton Residence, located on a busy waterfront road near Victoria, British Columbia, is a robust stucco-clad mass. The closed nature of the building, combined with its depression into the landscape, provides protection from the adjacent roadway. This largely inarticulate form is strategically carved away at both the south-west and the north-east corners. The resultant concavities provide a counterpoint to the building mass; a modulated venue to consolidate fenestration, points of access and egress, providing diverse opportunities for view and daylighting. Most importantly they define and qualify exterior space as an extension of interior volumes.

The front to back duplex defines its relationship to its site most notably in section. Desktops in the office are located level with the adjacent grade. Bamboo hedges, which share a scale commensurate with that of the dwelling, are used to mitigate views of neighbouring structures and define exterior spaces. Window head and sill heights, as well as floor levels, are modulated to express clear connections with both distant and immediate views.

On the waterfront in Vancouver's west side, the offset and elongated four-unit condominium development creates a staggered series of narrow courtyard spaces that provide relief from the constricted site. The board formed, concrete side walls of the building have limited fenestration, providing a relatively neutral backdrop for the heavily landscaped courts. This landscape becomes the foreground in views of the neighbouring buildings.

BattersbyHowat
Vancouver, British Columbia
www.battersbyhowat.com

David Battersby
b. 1968, Revelstoke, BC; B.ES. (Landscape) (Manitoba) 1989;
M.Arch. (TUNS) 1995.
Heather Howat
b. 1967, Flin Flon, MB; B.ID. (Manitoba) 1990; M.Arch. (TUNS) 1995.

Appleton Residence
Saanich, British Columbia 2003-2005
Project Team
Mary Cuk
Josie Grant
Chris Lee
Structural Engineer
Herold Engineering Ltd.
Geotechnical Engineer
CN Ryzuk and Associates Ltd.
Builder
Hemsworth Construction Ltd.
Photography
BattersbyHowat

Duplex
Vancouver, BC 2002-2005
Project Team
BattersbyHowat
Structural Engineer
Bevan-Pritchard Man Associates Ltd.
Photography
Martin Tessler

Fourplex
Vancouver, BC 2003-2005
Architect of Record
Hancock Bruckner Eng + Wright
Project Team
Mary Cuk
Jim Hancock
Chris Lee
Caroline Léveillé
Matthew McLeod
Craig Simms
Structural Engineer
Robertson, Kolbeins, Teevan, Gallaher Associates Ltd. (RKTG)
Geotechnical Engineer
United Pacific Geotechnical Engineering
Mechanical, Electrical Engineer
AC Mechanical Solutions Inc.

Code Consultant
Locke MacKinnon Domingo Gibson and Associates
Envelope Engineer
JRS Engineering Ltd.
Developer
JEL Investment & Briland Incorporated
Builder
Brandes Development Corporation
Photography
BattersbyHowat

PETER CARDEW
Morris and Helen Belkin Art Gallery
University of British Columbia, Vancouver

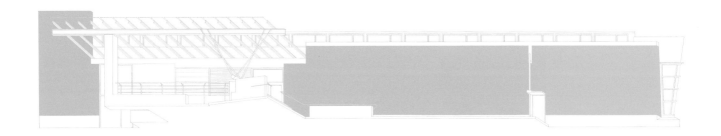

After the Vancouver Art Gallery, the Morris and Helen Belkin Art Gallery is the largest non-commercial gallery in the city. Located at one of the main entry points to the University of British Columbia, the building anchors the Fine Arts Precinct that comprises the Fine Arts Facility, the School of Music, the Frederick Wood Theatre and the School of Architecture. The siting and form of the building acknowledges both its formal role on the University Main Mall and its informal role as a catalyst for the differing disciplines of the Fine Arts Precinct.

Within the Gallery, the configuration of exhibition spaces can be changed using a system of large rotating walls to accommodate the spatial requirements of particular exhibitions. As an example, the exhibition of large powerful works by Canadian contemporary artist, Attila Richard Lukacs, was followed by an exhibition of small delicate works by the nineteenth century French Romantic painter, Theodore Gericault, without either exhibition being compromised by the spatial configuration of the building.

Unlike a civic gallery, the Belkin is a place of learning and research, and as such the curatorial and administrative functions are evident and accessible. A secondary, yet significant attribute of this openness and interaction, is the reduction in the personnel required for supervision.

By capturing views of the landscape from within the building, the intensity of the gallery experience is relieved, thereby encouraging longer and more contemplative visits.

Peter Cardew Architects
Vancouver, British Columbia
www.cardew.ca

Peter Cardew
b. 1939, Guildford, England; Dip.Arch. (Kingston Polytechnical), 1964.

Morris and Helen Belkin Art Gallery,
University of British Columbia
Vancouver, British Columbia 1995
Project Team
Marc Boutin
Janne Corniel
Don Kasko
Structural Engineer
C.Y. Loh Associates
Mechanical, Electrical Engineer
D.W. Thompson Consultants Ltd.
Drawings
Michael Kothke
Model Fabrication
Peter Wood
Client
University of British Columbia

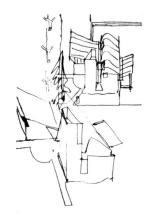

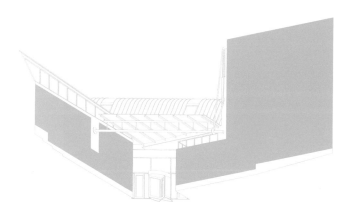

HOTSON BAKKER
KUWABARA PAYNE McKENNA BLUMBERG

Richmond City Hall

Located south of Vancouver on the delta of the Fraser River, Richmond was originally founded as a farming and fishing community. It is now one of British Columbia's fastest developing municipalities. Built on the original site of the 1919 Town Hall, the location of the new City Hall deliberately extends the tradition of civic meeting space in Richmond's history. However, the site itself is generally unexceptional and suburban in character, bounded by high-speed traffic corridors.

The City Hall forms an ensemble of buildings and landforms, which enclose a Civic Square and configure a network of landscaped outdoor courtyards and gardens. By breaking the project into three precincts, functional activities are clarified and flexibility in operations and environmental efficiency is maximized. At the forefront of the grouping, the circular Council Chamber is located at the south-east edge of the site in proximity to the street; its glazed perimeter encouraging accessibility and civic participation. Immediately to its north is an eight-storey Administrative Tower. The horizontal, two-storey Meeting House anchors the Council Chamber and the Tower on the east end, and extends west as the primary circulation spine through the site. Its glass and timber framed galleria projects to the exterior, defining primary entrances at the east and west ends. As the main organizing element, the Meeting House links interior programme components, as well as outdoor courtyard and gardens.

The design of the new City Hall plays a critical role in implementing the first step towards realizing Richmond's vision of creating a civic focus for the city. The landscaping and topography of the site play a pivotal role in establishing the public domain of this project. The landscape preserves existing heritage trees and maximizes the use of low-maintenance, local plant materials. The topography of cascading water features and extensive berming creates an abstracted network of landform and vegetation, evoking symbolic references to an indigenous terrain of dykes and sloughs. The overall integration of architecture and landscape transforms the site into an urban oasis.

Two fundamental ideas inform the design of Richmond City Hall:

1. The seamless integration of urban design, building design, sustainability and landscape design:

An urban collage of buildings and landscape elements establishes a specific framework for future on-site civic development, and models an ambitious possible urbanization for a rapidly unfolding suburban context.

The collection of eight-storey Administrative Tower (verticality), two-storey Meeting House (horizontality), and circular Council Chamber (punctuation), in combination with a parking plinth and metaphoric landscape of "dykes" frame a public domain of crisp civic plaza and verdant indigenous gardens.

The massing of the tower provides a landmark, and its solar orientation a healthy and light-filled workplace, minimizing energy use.

2. The melding of civic typological form with the topography of a specific place:

The current typology of city halls in Canada proposes ideas of civic architecture and the public realm. Rather than a singular building image, recent developments formulate urban ensembles that create a civic landscape. This strategy proposes a clear and formal articulation of the political, administrative and public functions of city halls. The conversation between these components creates an exterior realm for civic life.

The topography of place (climate, history, materiality, building technologies, local culture) infuses the local in Richmond City Hall. Delta conditions of high water tables and dykes are interwoven with the multi-ethnic cultural particularities of Richmond and Feng Shui. The Pacific North-West tradition of gardens is entwined with a reinterpreted 1950s West Coast modernism of timber, glass and concrete.

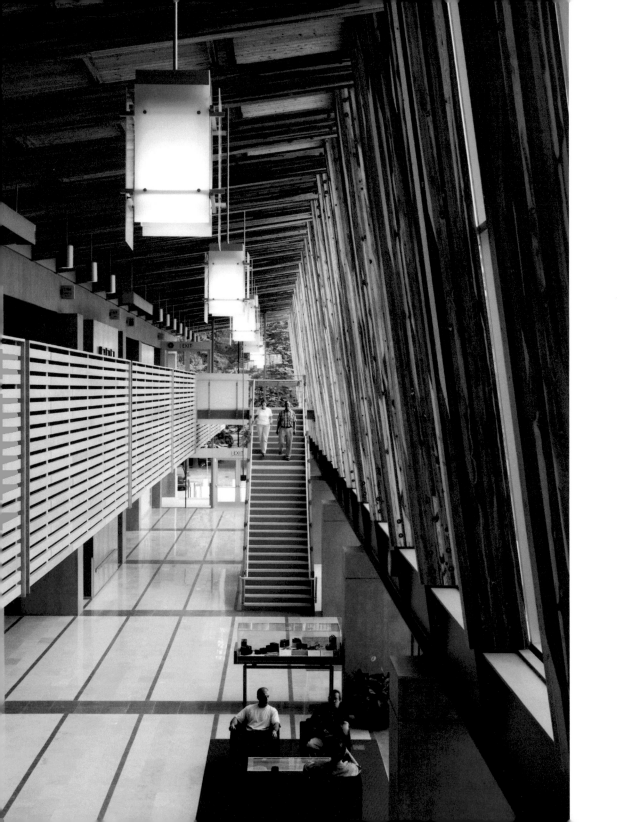

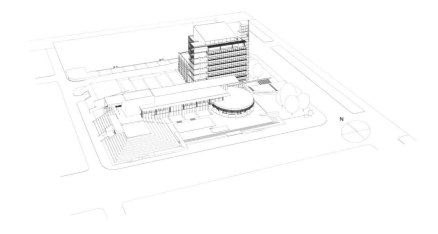

N

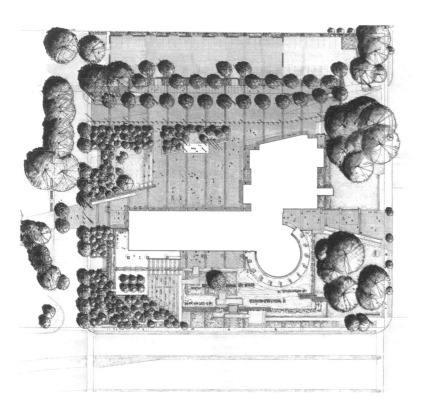

Hotson Bakker/Kuwabara Payne McKenna Blumberg
Associated Architects
Vancouver, British Columbia
www.hotsonbakker.com
www.kpmb.ca

Joost Bakker
b. 1945, Williamstad, Curaçao; B.A. (Toronto), 1967;
B.Arch. (Toronto), 1974.
Bruce Kuwabara
b. 1949, Hamilton; B.Arch. (Toronto), 1972.

Richmond City Hall
Richmond, BC 1998-2000
Project Team
Joyce Drohan
Rick Clarke
Kate Gerson
Andreas Kaminsky
Scott Edwards
Deryk Whitehead
Andre D'Elia
John Wall
Glen MacMullin
Judith Taylor
Bill Colaco
Neil Bauman
Structural Engineer
Bush, Bohlman & Partners
Mechanical Engineer
Stantec Consulting Ltd.
Electrical Engineer
R.A. Duff & Associates Inc.
Landscape
Phillips Farevaag Smallenberg Inc.
Sustainability
Gordon Shymko & Associates Inc.
Ray Cole
Audio-visual, Acoustics
BKL Consultants Ltd.
Feng Shui
Sherman Tai
Construction Management
Dominion Construction
Photography
Martin Tessler

HENRIQUEZ PARTNERS
IBI GROUP
BC Cancer Research Centre
Vancouver

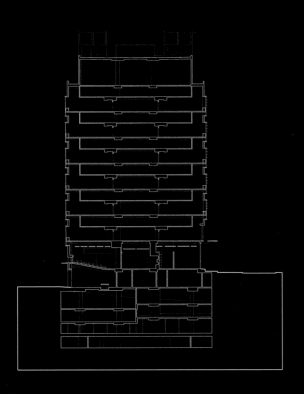

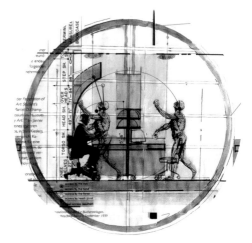

The BC Cancer Research Centre is the latest fully integrated state of the art Cancer Research Centre in Canada. It includes facilities for the Genome Sequence Centre, the first of its kind, dedicated to cancer research across the country. Located across the street and connected to the BC Cancer Treatment Centre, the facility will allow "benchtop" to "bedside" research and treatment, allowing a faster turnaround of information relating to promising new therapies.

The Centre is conceived as a two-building complex where researchers' offices are expressed as one building and the laboratories as another. The project will house six hundred scientists and staff, and is the first of two phases that will transform the entire city block. Laboratories are the heart of the building and make up 65 percent of its area. They are arranged in an open plan with modular bays—two or more typically used by each principal investigator and his or her team. The building also includes interstitial floors for ease of maintenance and flexibility. Offices and support spaces make up 20 percent of the space that includes a two hundred and twenty seat lecture theatre, seminar rooms, library, staff lounge, bicycle storage and shower facilities. The remaining 15 percent of the building consists of a large vivarium and support spaces.

A dominant feature is the set of large circular windows that flood the interior with natural light. Each window focuses on a group of researchers working behind their respective metaphorical "Petri dish." This becomes an expression of the cellular nature of individual research projects; each with a definite specialized focus but contributing to the main goal of finding a cure for cancer.

The office block is composed of two-floor suites serving each lab floor. Offices look out to ocean and mountain views through thin multi-coloured vertical strips. This coloured window treatment is an abstraction of a sequence of Chromosome 8, a subject of study in cancer research. A spiral "DNA" stair joins the office floors together. At the foot of the stair are small meeting rooms designed to encourage collaboration between researchers. Apart from its iconic function, the spiral staircase is envisioned as the setting for a proposed fundraising event, the "DNA Grind," inspired by Vancouver's popular outdoor exercise trail known as the "Grouse Grind."

Henriquez Partners
with IBI Group, Architect in joint venture
Vancouver, British Columbia
www.henriquezpartners.com

Richard Henriquez
b. 1941, Jamaica; B.Arch. (Manitoba), 1964;
M.Arch. (MIT), 1967.
David Thom
b. 1950, Toronto; B.Arch. (Toronto), 1974.

BC Cancer Research Centre
Vancouver, British Columbia
Project Team
Ivo Taller
Ron Eagleston
Daniel Friessen
Peter Lambur
Shawn LaPointe
Jason Martin
Raj Nath
Rui Nunes
Scott Posno

Christian Schimert
Frank Stebner
Peter Willems
Lab Consultant
Earl Walls Associates
Contractor
Ledcor Group
Structural Engineer
Glotman Simpson Group
Mechanical Engineer
Keen Engineering
Electrical Engineer
R.A. Duff & Associates Inc.
Programme and
Project Management
Stantec Consulting Ltd.
Landscape
Durante Kreuk Ltd.
Client
BC Cancer Foundation
Photography
Nic Lehoux

Overall Systems Design
Commercial, Renfrew and Rupert Stations

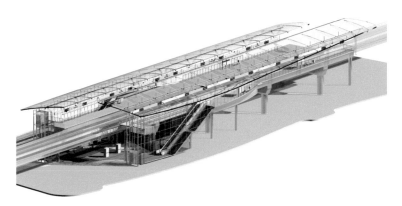

The 20 kilometre Millennium Line is the latest addition to the Lower Mainland's SkyTrain rapid transit system that opened in August 2002. Like the original 26 kilomtre Expo Line, the Millennium Line is an automated rapid transit system operating on a grade-separated guide-way, featuring twelve new stations along an emerging industrial corridor. The SkyTrain system first opened in January 1986, to coincide with Expo 86. Although it has carried more than five hundred million passengers since then, steady population growth through the late 1980s and 1990s in the north-eastern portions of the region created the need for system expansion.

Development of the Millennium Line involved a number of design and engineering innovations. Designed by some of Vancouver's leading architects, the stations feature extensive use of glass to create bright and safe public spaces. Each station is designed to reflect the character of its neigh-bourhood, resulting in a series of structures that are architecturally distinct and provide an appealing alternative to the private automobile.

As lead architects, VIA Architecture defined the overall design informed by local response, using a systems approach that established consistency throughout the project. By organizing system-wide elements such as station furniture, signage, and monitoring systems into a legible and coherent design family, the individual station architects were freed to express specific formal approaches that respond to local community and physical settings, most commonly through the articulation of station canopy structures. The play between these "elements of continuity" and the "elements of distinction" resulted in a group of stations that are variations on a common theme, using individual architectural design for differentiation.

Three primary station typologies were established: "Landmark" Stations (such as Brentwood Station by Busby + Associates); "Urban Infill" Stations (such as Commercial, Rupert and Renfrew Stations by VIA Architecture); and "Place Maker" Stations (such as Lake City by Walter Francl/Stantec), intended to inspire future development in the area surrounding the stations.

Our design process continued a long tradition of collaboration between architectural firms on large projects in Vancouver. Expo 86, Simon Fraser University and False Creek illustrate the strength of this architectural synergy, where architects chosen for their design ability and sensitivity to project needs create a whole that is greater than the sum of its parts.

VIA Architecture
Vancouver, British Columbia
www.via-architecture.com

Alan Hart
b. 1952, Halifax; B.A. (McGill), 1974; B.Arch. (UBC), 1978.
Graham McGarva
b. 1952, Scotland; B.A. Arch. (Cambridge), 1973;
M.A. Arch. (Cambridge), 1977; B.Arch. (UBC), 1978.

Millenium SkyTrain Line – Overall System Design;
Commercial, Renfrew and Rupert Stations
Greater Vancouver, British Columbia 2002
Project Team
Dale Rickard
Catherine Hart
Andrew Norrie
Edward LeFlufy
Keir Robinson
Dimitri Harvalias
Charlene Kovacs
Walter Schnurrenberger
Eric Stedman
Glen Stokes (system-wide elements)
Structural Engineer
Glotman-Simpson
Fast + Epp Structural Engineers
Mechanical Engineer
Keen Engineering
Electrical Engineering
Sandwell Engineering Inc.
Landscape
Durante Kreuk Ltd.
Client
Rapid Transit Project 2000
Photography
Ed White

WALTER FRANCL/STANTEC
Millennium SkyTrain Line,
Greater Vancouver
Lake City Station

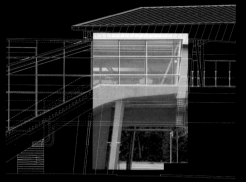

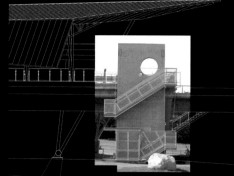

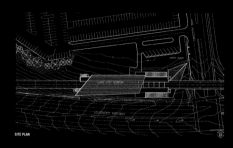

SITE PLAN

Lake City Station is located at the intersection of Lake City Way, the entrance to a "high-tech" business park currently under construction, and the Lougheed Highway, a busy arterial route cresting in elevation to the east and falling away, west of the station. Seen from an eastern approach, along Lougheed, the station appears to climb from the ground; approached from the west, it appears as dramatically hovering. The immediate site, under and adjacent to the station, is simply a sloping lawn that climbs to the north, away from the highway. South of the station, immediately across the Lougheed Highway, is a continuous stand of mixed, mature deciduous and coniferous trees with an established residential neighbourhood beyond.

The station is conceived as a wind-swept cloud, a dynamic Japanese origami-like shroud that is anchored to the ground at its eastern end and leaping cantilevered above the ground to the west. It aspires to frozen dynamism and technological ambition. As a gateway structure, it affirms the character of the high-tech park it fronts. Steel—painted, gavalume finished and stainless—combined with glass, aluminum and concrete comprise the spare, long-lasting materials of the station's construction. Oval, darkly pigmented "Agilia" concrete, platform-support columns form the base of the superstructure, and are canted seven degrees to the west, as are the sandblasted

concrete fin walls supporting the stairs and escalators. The concrete base of the entry canopy and structural steel columns, springing from the top of the base to support the canopy, cant dramatically. The steel trusses of the platform roof canopies taper in depth and are framed in a diagonal bias to the sideway and platforms. The stair/escalator roof structure is framed high above the traveller's head at the concourse level, and pinches to a minimum at this platform level. A tall, angled "V" column strut surmounts a canted concrete base, stretching skyward to support what seems to be an impossibly long cantilever of the upper roof's west end. In places, horizontal window mullions are seemingly stretched beyond their fixing points by speed itself. All of these compositional elements are intended to reinforce the spirit of a dynamic search for technological invention and lend this spirit to SkyTrain travel.

The client's ambitions for the design of the Millennium Line stations were threefold: to build a significant, regionally identifiable portal to the neighbourhoods through which the train passes; to provide a safe, transparent refuge for the traveller; and to construct stations that were durable and long-lasting. The project treads as lightly as possible on the landscape and wherever possible the site was returned to its preconstruction state. The landscaping was designed to require no irrigation, other than that falling from the sky.

Walter Francl Architect Inc.
with Stantec Architecture in joint venture
Vancouver, British Columbia
www.wfrancl.com

Walter Francl
b. 1952, Vienna; B.Sc.Eng. (Alberta), 1975; B.Arch. (UBC), 1979; M.Arch. (Harvard), 1986.
Peter Buchanan
b. 1955, Toronto; B.Arch. (Carleton), 1988.

Millenium SkyTrain Line –
Lake City Station
Burnaby, BC 2002
Project Team
Neville Doyle
Ken Tsai
David Harding
Eric Pettit
Structural Engineer
C.Y. Loh and Associates
Mechanical, Electrical Engineer
Earth Tech (Canada) Inc.
Builder
Westpro Constructors Group Ltd.
Landscape
Phillips Farevaag Smallenberg
Public Art
Metaform
Client
Rapid Transit Project 2000
Photography
Joaquin Pedrero
Walter Francl Architect
Edward White
Stantec Architecture

BUSBY + ASSOCIATES
Millennium SkyTrain Line, Greater Vancouver
Brentwood Station

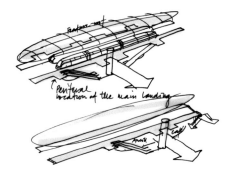

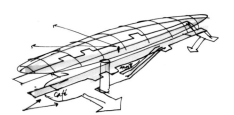

Employing elements of clear, open spaces—using glass for visibility and the provision of generous canopies for rain and wind protection—the Brentwood Station was designed to encourage the use of the transit system, through accessibility, safety and comfort. The site's proximity to an existing bus loop to the north makes the station a major transfer point. Straddling the Lougheed Highway and adjacent to parking for the Brentwood Mall, the highly visible Brentwood Station was conceived as a major focal point in this area of the city.

The main structural elements supporting the outer shell are a series of curved composite ribs set five metres apart: the lower (wall) section being steel and the upper (roof) portion glue-laminated timber. The ribs of the two canopies are connected via a structural gutter to steel cross-bracing and V-shaped steel struts that create a system of moment frames and transfer lateral loads across the central void. The complementary properties of steel and wood dictate the architectural language: steel in exposed locations and wood where protected from the weather. Above the glazing, traditional technology takes over; the roof being constructed of 38 millimetre × 89 millimetre members laid on edge and spiked together. It was the skill of the craftsmen and the flexibility of the material that enabled the decking to follow the changing geometry of the roof, creating the inverted "hardwood floor" effect.

Transit stations are, by their very nature, green buildings—their main function is to reduce vehicular traffic and carbon dioxide emissions. In the design of Brentwood Station, an effort was made to be as environmentally responsible as possible within the comprehensive guidelines laid out by the client. The green strategies that were employed concerned site conservation, natural illumination and ventilation, energy conservation, water conservation, sustainable materials, and alternative transportation strategies (including bicycle storage for commuter convenience). The striking form of the structure will hopefully convince more commuters to leave their automobiles at home.

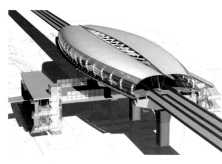

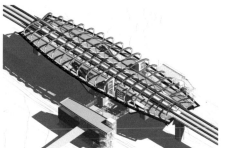

Busby + Associates Architects
(now Busby Perkins + Will Architects, Co.)
Vancouver, British Columbia
www.busbyperkinswill.ca

Peter Busby
b. 1952, Southport, England; B.A. (Toronto), 1974;
B.Arch. (UBC), 1977.
David Dove
b. 1963, Vancouver; B.A. (SFU), 1989; B.Arch. (UBC), 1992.
Martin Nielsen
b. 1963, Lagos, Nigeria; B.A.Sc. (UBC), 1986; M.Arch. (UBC), 1996.
Brian Wakelin
b. 1970, Victoria; B.Sc. (Victoria), 1992; M.Arch. (UBC), 1998.

Millennium SkyTrain Line – Brentwood Station
Burnaby, BC 2002
Project Team
Brian Billingsley
Marco Bonaventura
Scott Edwards
Teryl Mullock
Richard Peck
Soren Schou
Adam Slawinski

Structural Engineer
Fast & Epp Partners
Mechanical Engineer
Klohn Crippen
Electrical Engineering
Agra Simons Ltd.
Landscape Architect
Durante Kreuk Ltd.
Public Artist
Jill Anholt
Client
Rapid Transit Project 2000
Photography
Nic Lehoux

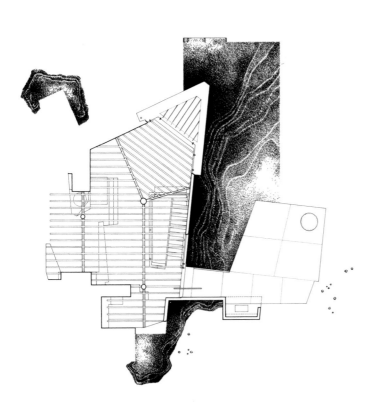

Patkau Architects, Barnes House, Nanaimo

RESTRUCTURING THE DISCUSSION OF CONTEMPORARY ARCHITECTURE
Andrew Gruft

Before embarking on any discussion of Canadian architecture, one of the first and most obvious questions that ought to be addressed is what does one mean by the term? What possible range of meanings might the category *Canadian architecture* have? Here I do not mean simple problems of definition such as whether it would comprise work done by Canadians anywhere, or only work done by Canadians in Canada (the scope of this exhibition), but rather how one might usefully construct this concept. For this leads into broader and much more complex issues involving ideas of national identity, the very ones that always give Canadians such difficulty. The underlying question remains, is there really any point in using the nation as a unit of organization for the discussion of architecture? My belief in its value is a position opposed to much current thinking, given the generally uncritical acceptance of the idea that culture has been globalized, rendering the study of architecture by nation largely irrelevant.

I thought Canada was a cultural unity of some considerable importance if one wished to explore deeper issues, beyond the explicit individual differences of design approach or building form: there were recurring themes that were implicit in the work of a wide variety of practitioners in this country. I had worked on this topic some twenty years previously during the preparation of an exhibition of Canadian architecture titled *A Measure of Consensus: Canadian Architecture in Transition*, which described the change in underlying attitudes that had taken place in projects being designed in the mid-1980s, as opposed to those of the previous twenty years. I felt that such shared attitudes owed much to the common cultural context provided by this place, Canada: a shared history, common experience and similar working conditions all seemed significant determinants of this commonality. This evidence of a set of common characteristics underlying Canadian architecture, which appeared to change over time, provided an important reason to pursue the national perspective.

Rather than looking for a simplistic similarity of appearance to characterize national architecture—something that is found in traditional peasant cultures before the advent of modernism, but doesn't survive within the contemporary communications network of global culture—I felt the study of this underlying set of characteristics to be the correct level at which to try to define a Canadian architecture. This seemed the only way in which such a term could have serious meaning: the common themes and characteristics that derive from shared values, attitudes and concerns common to work produced in the socio-geopolitical environment of this country Canada, the political entity, the nation state. And as Alan Colquhoun has suggested: "The materials of culture are similar in all cases, but each country tends to interpret these materials in a slightly different way. It is precisely because the ingredients of contemporary architecture are so similar all over the 'developed' world that the slight differences of interpretation to which they are subjected in different countries are so interesting."[1] Interesting and important—the differences of interpretation are not that slight, and the variance in attitude underlying them is significant. They reveal the culturally bound set of values that fundamentally affect architectural practice, and ultimately determine its range of possibilities, its spectrum or palette.

My position required some sort of conceptual underpinning. I proceeded to develop a working construct, a binary concept of *underlying structure/formal strategy*. With this I propose to structure the discussion of contemporary architecture on two interrelated levels: one which looks for common underlying themes and characteristics using the nation state as the socio-geopolitical unit of analysis; the other that proposes an analysis organized by design strategy and formal expression. The latter would be explored through what I call its *milieu*—a grouping of practitioners on the basis of the similarity or relatedness of design ideas, their formal characteristics and means of representation. Nowadays, such groupings tend to be international, though there are some notable exceptions that are local or regional: for example, in the Ticino.

Here, of course, the old Canadian problem of the region versus the nation rears its venerable head—one of the recurring themes of Canadian political and cultural life. Can one talk about Canada as a whole at all, or does one have to always consider it as an agglomeration of very different regions? I didn't think this was a critical problem for my position; I considered these to be hierarchically interconnected levels of the same socio-geopolitical web and would encourage work at both these levels, even exploring finer differentiation where required.

1. All quotations are from Alan Colquhoun's "Regionalism and Technology" reprinted in *Modernity and the Classical Tradition: Architectural Essays*, 1980-1987 (Cambridge, Mass. and London: MIT Press, 1989).

The question of how to study architecture is never simple—even the usual, regular categories are in doubt. What aggregations, what units of analysis should be used for discussion is a difficult issue. Such structures are, of course, not absolute; the selection of units and the construction of categories are relative, depending on what one seeks to learn. All groupings are problematic; it's never straightforward to predict the arrangement that will give the best results. Traditionally, various groupings have been used: by trend, movement or style; by patronage, power and influence; by historical period; by geographical area, region or nation. Grouping by country or nation seems to have fallen into disrepute lately, undermined by arguments about the globalization of culture and a suspicion of nationalistic metanarratives. Still echoing with unfortunate resonances of the horrendous events of recent memory, they have also been marginalized by the upsurge of an exaggerated individualism and the culture of celebrity.

It is my intention here to recuperate this category of "national architectures," which I believe to be potentially much more useful than is currently realized. The country or nation state is far too important as a unit of architectural analysis to be abandoned for the wrong reasons. The key point to be made here is that *an interest in national architectures does not necessarily imply a belief in national forms*. This long running confusion amongst architects stems from some form of misplaced concreteness: the naïve but persistent architectural belief that every culture can be expressed through its own consistent set of forms; one that embodies in some simplistic way the spirit of the place, the *genius locii* so beloved of the proponents of regionalism.

But such conditions are only present in the vernacular architecture of pre-modern peasant societies, where the isolation maintained by the lack of modern communication and industrialization ensures their continuity. Here, the consistent use of local forms, materials and ways of building are passed down from generation to generation, usually through an oral tradition. Few such uncontaminated situations exist any longer, and those that do are everyday being weakened by the inroads of international capitalism, or exist as artificially protected enclaves, living museums of past traditions maintained by government grants.

In those modern societies where there does seem to be a regional consistency of architectural form, such as the Ticino, it is clearly attributable to what I have called the *milieu*. This is a self-conscious intellectual grouping of architects who are working on a commonly agreed set of problems using a shared set of strategies, and are conscious of their common stance. These are inevitably supported by a school and set of teaching offices. One of the key indicators of such a situation is the choice of a self-consciously selected, limited palette of modern industrial materials—concrete block is clearly not a building material indigenous to the Italian/Swiss border!

Nowadays, the *milieu* is much more likely to be an international one, its location on the pages of a specific group of magazines and websites, and a particular set of conferences and lecture circuits. It comprises a series of practitioners united by common architectural preoccupations and formal strategies, and almost always a group of critics interested in propagating them. These may be located in a variety of places around the world linked by the lively international culture of architecture, and spurred on by the voracious architectural media that scours the world looking for fresh fodder for its readers to consume.

The choice of form is not just a matter of free will that allows one to decide what design approach to take, like choosing which cookies to buy in a supermarket. As in the supermarket, there are a series of underlying factors that determine the range of choice available. The set of ideas and strategies available—those that get to be considered by the individual designer—are always restricted, predetermined by a series of cultural and economic factors. It is precisely these issues that appear to be accessible via a study of architectural practice by nation.

Because the salient characteristics of the architecture of a specific place are not explicit but hidden, they are not easy to identify, but when found they are arguably even more interesting than the more obvious but varied formal characteristics. As mentioned earlier, they consist of the common preoccupations and the recurring themes underlying the variety of formal manifestations of the architecture of any given area. I argue that these are most affected by political/cultural divisions, of which the most mundane as well as the most powerful and obvious is still the nation state (as well as its subsets, the regions, the provinces or municipalities of which it is constituted). These are still the units with the most legal and administrative power, which determine the framework of rules and regulations, codes and specifications that architects work within. The nation state is still the most important economic unity, only challenged by the international corporation, and although no longer the complete master of its own fate, it still has the power to significantly affect or circumscribe activity. And most importantly, in cultural terms, I believe the same to be the case—shared histories and experience leave indelible marks on the people of a country, affecting and shaping cultural values, attitudes and points of view far more strongly than one realizes.

Common values and preoccupations manifest themselves in many different ways, expressed through a variety of formal strategies and design approaches. To combine serious critical discussion of formal issues with those of underlying values and attitudes one needs a working construct that integrates these issues in a way that would simultaneously account for a variety of architectural issues at a number of interrelated levels. A useful way of doing this is to recognize two complementary levels of investigation, two environments of operation: that of the *milieu* for the study of formal strategy, and that of the nation state as the socio-geopolitical unit of analysis for underlying structures. These are not mutually exclusive, but rather interconnected areas of study, which could give us a more comprehensive and profound understanding of current architectural practice.

Alan Colquhoun alludes to a similar categorization in his article, "Regionalism and Technology." He proposes a unit of analysis based on "the most obvious and banal divisions of the modern political world, in which the nation state is a reality. It is a regionalism based on politics…the result of a complex interaction between modern international capitalism and various national traditions ingrained in institutions and attitudes." He argues that it is at the level of the political entity of the nation state that one may find the subtle differences in attitude, revealing "…the unconscious ideologies underlying current practice [which are] connected with the actual political economic situation…."

Colquhoun uses a comparison of British and American skyscraper projects as an example to demonstrate the differences in attitude towards the relationship between architecture and technology. He describes the North American attitude to technology as pragmatic, compared with the idealistic attitude of Europe. He points out that the American examples are concerned with external configuration and surface, citing examples by Gordon Bunshaft, Cesar Pelli, Philip Johnson and Michael Graves. In contrast, he characterizes the European examples as expressive structures celebrating the idea of technological progress and suggesting a technological utopia, supporting his argument with the examples of the Hong Kong and Shanghai Bank by Norman Foster, and Lloyds of London by Rogers, and the Pompidou Centre by Renzo Piano and Richard Rogers. "…[T]he interest of this example lies in the fact that it suggests a connection between a certain kind of architecture and a certain kind of national consciousness. It is difficult not to draw the inference that the approach to technology in relation to architecture is influenced by deep-seated national obsessions."

It is precisely this sort of work that develops and gives greater depth to our architectural discourse, which somehow seems to have got stuck on specific discussions of individual architects. No matter how interesting these may be, we need a better understanding of the environment, of their ideas, and the background of the issues that underlie our formally varied architecture, and unconsciously shape our architectural production, against which their work can be discussed. This is what research on the identifiable characteristics of Canadian architecture would provide. It is also important to bring these hidden issues into the open so that we can at least be conscious of what informs our work. Architects might take positions on these issues, and we could even get competing factions arguing their relative merits in public and the architectural press, based on a more solid grounding in content uncovered by research. Such knowledge might allow us to foment a lively and stimulating debate as to what would be a more or less appropriate basis for our architecture. Perhaps even more important for architectural culture, this knowledge provides a potential way back into politics. It is at this level of discussion where the specifically architectural could intersect with the quotidian interests and political concerns of the general populace. Here is found the level of discourse at which connections might be made back into political life and through this the possibility of regained influence over the form of the city.

ANDREW GRUFT is currently Professor Emeritus in the School of Architecture at UBC, and one of the coordinators of the architectural lecture series of the Vancouver League. His field of interest and expertise has always been contemporary architecture and urban design, with a specific focus on Canada, the Americas, and Europe. He curated *A Measure of Concensus,* a survey of Canadian architecture, for the UBC Fine Arts Gallery in 1986; he has curated other architectural exhibitions, including a series at Vancouver's NOVA Gallery in 1981 (where he was co-owner and co-curator), and *Idea into Form,* which was shown at the UBC Fine Arts Gallery in 1983. He is the author of "Vancouver Architecture: The Last Fifteen Years," which appeared in the Vancouver Art Gallery catalogue, *Vancouver: Art and Artists: 1931-1983;* the catalogue for the *A Measure of Consensus* exhibition; the catalogue for *Patkau Architects, Projects: 1978-1990,* an exhibition that travelled through North America and Europe; fifteen entries on Canadian architects for the *Dictionnaire d'architecture de xxieme siecle* published by Hazan of Paris in 1997; and the monograph on Patkau Architects published by Gustavo Gili of Barcelona in 1997. Over the last few years, he has been working on a book concerning issues in Canadian architecture; a work which informs the conceptual basis of the exhibition, *Substance Over Spectacle.*

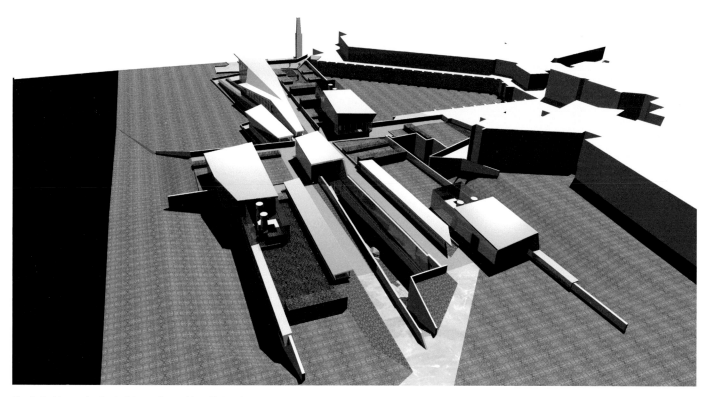

Teeple Architects, Academic Science Centre, Trent University

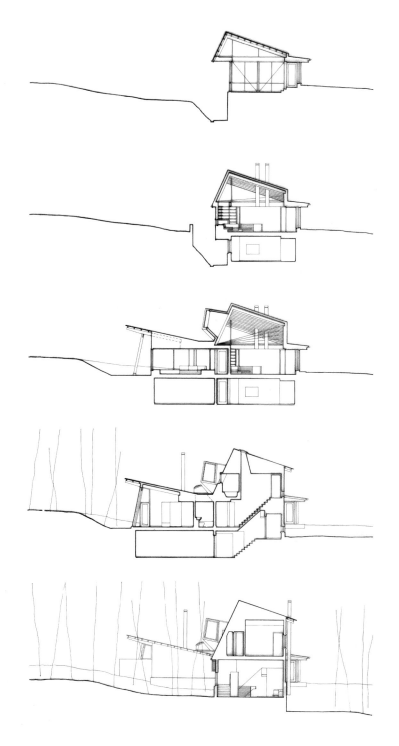

Ian MacDonald, House, Mulmur Hills

THE *AUTEUR*
IN CANADIAN ARCHITECTURE
George Baird

During the early planning stages of this book and exhibition, Andrew Gruft and I had a number of conversations about its theme. Among other things, we pondered the putative "Canadianness" of architecture in this country, as well as the role that Canadian architecture and Canadian commentators on architecture had played on the world stage in recent years. As it happened, I had already published responses to such questions in an Italian academic journal some three years ago.[1] Gruft was evidently intrigued enough by the views I expressed to ask me to amplify them in a contribution to this book.

I start with the matter of the putative "image" of Canadian architecture in the world at large. I had suggested that, as far as I could tell, it did not have a particularly strong one. To the extent that Canadian architects were visible internationally, they were known as individual firms, rather than as Canadians per se. John and Patricia Patkau, Saucier + Perrotte and Shim-Sutcliffe, in particular, come readily to my mind as firms that have received discriminating international recognition. And, as far as I can tell from my Toronto vantage point, firms such as Diamond and Schmitt and Kuwabara Payne McKenna Blumberg (KPMB) have also achieved acclaim. These two latter, large firms have obtained important commissions outside of Canada's borders that are of a scale that the previously mentioned three firms—despite their reputations—would find it difficult to compete for.

But I do not think any of the work of such firms are seen outside the country as "national" achievements. Nor do I believe the accomplishments of American, French or German architects are seen that way outside their national borders. It is probably the case that only Dutch architecture is seen outside of the Netherlands as being quintessentially "Dutch," and this is probably as much the result of the intense promotional support Dutch architects have received from the government of the Netherlands, as it is of any inherent body of architectural ideas they share.

Given my view of the "image" of Canadian architecture internationally, it will probably come as no surprise to the reader that I also believe that none of the firms I have just cited would qualify as "stars." Indeed, perhaps the only Canadian working in a design field who would qualify as an international "star" is the graphic designer, Bruce Mau. But again, it should be emphasized that the star system (with the possible exception of the Dutch) doesn't have much to do with nationality; instead, in its focus on charismatic, individual celebrity, the international star system can barely assimilate partnerships of architects, let alone national groups of them.

Thus I can perhaps acknowledge that Canadian architects do have one feature in common: none of them is a participant in the star system. Admired abroad though they are, neither the Patkaus, nor Saucier + Perrotte, nor Shim-Sutcliffe qualify as stars, in the manner of Frank Gehry, Zaha Hadid, Rem Koolhaas, or Daniel Libeskind. Then again, are Canadians in other cultural spheres viewed differently? It is probably true that Vancouver artist, Jeff Wall, is a "star" in the international art world, but I do not think Alice Munro or Mavis Gallant (my two favourite Canadian authors) would qualify as such. And, if we move to the cinema, I don't think that Denys Arcand, David Cronenberg or Atom Egoyan would either, even though these directors are admired as cinematic *auteurs*.

With the citation of this term from film history, I have perhaps come upon a productive analogy. For the "*auteur* theory," as it eventually came to be known in the history of film in the twentieth century, was an invention of young French film critics and directors who had long admired the work of a group of American film directors, including John Ford, Howard Hawks and Alfred Hitchcock. Conventional film criticism characterized these figures as commercial journeymen, capable enough, no doubt, but held hostage to the studio system, and incapable of producing high cinematic art. Not so, insisted the young French revisionists. Instead, the young partisans of *Cahiers du Cinema* vigorously defended the characteristic modes of filming of these figures, insisting that the thematic continuity that could be traced from individual film to individual film in the work of each was one of the things that made the films compelling. It was, in fact, this thematic continuity that prompted the French to name their heroes *auteurs*. Is it possible that among the Canadian architects whom I argue cannot be considered "stars," there are some who can be considered *auteurs*? In my view, the answer is yes, and since Gruft has chosen to represent some of the firms in the show by groups of projects, the possibility exists for me to treat a few of them in a fashion parallel to that of the young French writers of *Cahiers*. This is not to suggest that the three

Brian MacKay-Lyons, Howard House, West Pennant

I will discuss in detail are the only ones capable of being treated in this way. It would clearly be possible to deal with Saucier + Perrotte or Shim-Sutcliffe or the Patkaus in a parallel way—it is just that they are not, in the present exhibition, as conveniently represented by groups of related projects, as are Brian MacKay-Lyons, Ian MacDonald and architectsAlliance.

Let me begin with the work of MacKay-Lyons. It is possible, from a point early in his career, to trace a strong thread of typological evolution. His renovation of a two hundred year-old house on the Nova Scotia coast is a good starting point. By definition typological, as it takes an existing historic building as its point of departure, it also creates a number of engaging counter-themes. First, the interior volume of the existing building is almost entirely evacuated, giving to its envelope a presence even greater than the one it originally had. Then, a sizeable, formal volume is inserted into the void of the existing volume. This insertion penetrates the roof, marks new interior spatial divisions, and provides structural bracing to the entire complex. Partly revealing and partly counter-pointing the building's historic status, this lighthouse-like form enables us to read the project's overall typological references in a long historical continuum.

In the case of the Rubadoux-Cameron house from a few years later, an entirely new building strongly reiterates a volumetric form that is locally both typological and historic: an elementary rectangular volume surmounted by a simple, relatively steeply pitched roof. The type is initially posited in virtually Rationalist concept-ual terms. As with Robert Venturi's Trubek and Wislocki Houses (1970-1971), the historicizing implications of the primary volume of the building are engagingly undercut by the deliberately ahistorical pattern of window openings in the skin. This mannerist pictorial undercurrent in the appearance of the house renders the tautness of the building skin more palpable than it would otherwise be.

By the time he gets to the Yaukey Cottage (1991), Brian MacKay-Lyons' local, hist-orical typological referent has shifted somewhat, from residential historical struc-tures to more industrial ones. Barns and sheds are invoked more frequently in his work, but this does not mean that the "*auteur-like*" consistency of the work is sharply attenuated. The elementary volumes are almost as strong as they always were; the one-to-one relationship of structural systems and skin still provides the primary interior spatial order of the buildings, while the material palette continues to emphasize tautness of skin.

In MacKay-Lyons' more recent works, such as the Howard House (1995) and the House on the Nova Scotia Coast #22 (1997), a further interesting shift occurs: in these larger and more complex residential projects, the building programmes are broken out into semi-separate building volumes. Yet despite this, the overall compositions of these buildings still posit unified conceptual volumes. In these later cases, complex combinations of solids and voids make up the overall unified figures that these buildings present so compellingly on the land. These later examples of MacKay-Lyons' houses manage to be both big and little at the same time.

Equally typological, although in respect to a different repertoire of formal themes, is the work of Toronto architect Ian MacDonald. Like MacKay-Lyons, MacDonald's work is largely made up of residential projects for private clients. Still, MacDonald's work has a number of points of departure distinct from those of the Nova Scotia architect. First, elementary volumes are of much less formal significance to MacDonald than they are to MacKay-Lyons. MacDonald is clearly not influenced by Rationalism. It is widely agreed that his work is typified by sets of shifting and sliding planes reminiscent of de Stijl, the work of Ron Thom and, of course, Frank Lloyd Wright. Second, in a characteristically rambling, hugging relationship to the landscapes they occupy, MacDonald's houses present more complex and obscured visual impressions to the approaching visitor. Formally, volumetrically and spatially, they are only gradually apprehended by such a visitor over time as he or she moves around the exterior and interior spaces created by the design. If the narratives evoked by MacKay-Lyons' projects can be described as historical/conceptual, MacDonald's are instead cinematic, sequential, pictorial.

Two of MacDonald's houses from 1999 illustrate these themes compellingly. The Deacon Kravis House and the house in Mulmur Hills have approximately "L-shaped" plans, and in both the pivot of the "L" is the kitchen. In each house one arm accommodates the public functions, while the other is private. But the perimeters of the "L's" in both houses are irregular, incorporating a series of intermediate scale syncopations that form, among other features, bay windows, covered entrances and exits, and inglenooks.

In the sections of MacDonald's houses, another set of syncopations comes into play. This set is initially posited by a juxtaposition of a strongly expressed set of horizontal data: roofs, window heads, tops of retaining walls, and the much more plastic forms of pitched roofs and overhangs. As a result, the slipping and overlapping volumetrics so typical of MacDonald find expression in section as well as in plan. What is more, the undulations of the roof forms link the buildings explicitly back to analogous undulations of the land forms within and upon which they sit.

Brian MacKay-Lyons, House on the Nova Scotia Coast #22

In perhaps his most accomplished work to date—the house he recently completed for himself and his family in Toronto's legendary Wychwood Park—MacDonald brings the entire repertoire of characteristic themes of his work into sharp focus. The project is a renovation of a modest bungalow that was unaccountably and inexplicably erected in the 1960s in the middle of the celebrated "Arts and Crafts" precinct from the early twentieth century. Wychwood is now a heritage conservation district, and the bungalow would never be approved for construction today. Accordingly, MacDonald was only allowed to modify the house within a highly constraining set of municipal restrictions. As a result, he was obliged to undertake his customary performance of shifting planes and sliding volumetric relationships of building elements within a much more decisively demarcated overall pictorial frame of reference than is usually the case in his work. His design strategy was to construct additional building elements both outwards and downwards from the form of the existing building, allowing the original bungalow roof to remain (both literally and figuratively) as the unifying and completing form of the overall composition.

Another Toronto firm, architectsAlliance, deserves attention for a series of projects commissioned by Howard Cohen of Context Developments. Unlike the projects of MacKay-Lyons and MacDonald, these works of architectsAlliance entirely comprise commercial development projects for residential condominiums. Commercial design projects for similar programmes are usually inescapably typological in character, so perhaps that aspect of these projects is not so surprising. But two not so typical things can also be said about them. First, that they are all of an unusually high level of design quality. For years, I have been envious of, and embarrassed by, the high quality of commercial residential design work in Vancouver compared with similar projects in Toronto, but with the advent of Cohen as developer, and Alliance as architects, the design quality of multiple residential building projects in Toronto has begun to improve. Peter Clewes, the Alliance partner in charge of the projects for Context, has been described as an admirer of Peter Dickinson (the highly regarded Toronto architect of the late 1950s and early 1960s—many of his projects were multiple-residential buildings for commercial clients). Clewes seems to have adopted Dickinson's highly creative way of dealing with the unavoidable expediency of commercial architecture.

The second thing to be said about the Alliance/Context projects is that, like those of MacDonald, they present an interesting repertoire of formal strategies. Some of the buildings have been designed with access decks; some with through units; some with skip floor corridors (facilitating the provision of through units even within a more-or-less conventional, double-loaded corridor cross-section). Recently, most of them have taken the form of more conventional high-rise towers, but efforts are always made in these cases to maximize slenderness and to minimize bulk.

architectsAlliance, Radio City, Toronto

The power of the Context projects lies not in programmatic/formal variability, but in Alliance's skill at deploying the characteristic material palette of residential building skins to create powerful plastic effects—whether in a slab-block format like at MOZO, or a tower format at Radio City, the volumes of the building forms are always organized to maximize the relationship of sheer surfaces of glass, articulating residential balconies and the solid elements comprising vertical circulation elements. In these projects, the balcony balustrades are usually glass, establishing a strong link between these elements and the taut, glazed skins of the buildings' primary volumes. But the solid elements vary from project to project, depending on the required degree of contrast to the glazed surfaces, the material palette of adjacent existing buildings, and the extent to which the solid volumes are intended to "float." At District Lofts and MOZO, brick is employed to anchor the buildings to the ground plane, while at Radio City, pre-cast concrete panels cause the building to hover above it. In each of these projects, the compositional play achieved with such elements is extended upwards, creating the most engaging relationships of primary building volumes to roofscapes seen in Toronto on commercial residential building projects in many years.

I profoundly enjoy the complex sets of relations visible in the work of these three architects. It is gratifying to savour the growing tectonic precision and mature typological approach these designers demonstrate in their work. In their systematic exploration of interrelated building issues over a series of design projects, these designers have managed to construct a design culture that is admittedly not spectacularized, but is nonetheless deep, resonant and worthy of being pleasurably pondered over time.

So I find myself supposing that perhaps it doesn't matter that Canadian architects lack charismatic international profiles—in particular, that it is not their "Canadianness" that strikes foreigners as their most important feature. After all, this is probably true for the writers, Mavis Gallant and Alice Munro, and for the filmmakers, Arcand, Cronenberg and Egoyan as well. As I remarked three years ago to my Italian colleague, Francesco Garofalo, who was worried that Italian architects nowadays didn't seem to be all that visible in the global media either, perhaps Canadians would be well advised to make the best of a local situation, so long as

architectsAlliance, MoZo, Toronto

it is one in which we are interested in the work of our peers, and they are interested in ours, creating a discourse that can be kept afloat, manifesting difference and commonality in mutually provocative ways.

The text is adapted from an interview that was published in *Quaderni PPC*, no. 2, 2002, by the School of Architecture at the University of Pescara. The issue was edited by Lorenzo Pignatti and devoted to the theme of architecture in Canada.

GEORGE BAIRD graduated from the University of Toronto in 1962. In 1964, he commenced graduate studies in architecture at University College, London, England, and went on to teach architectural theory and design at the Royal College of Art, and the Architectural Association School of Architecture. In 1967, he returned to Toronto, and in 1968, opened his own architectural practice and joined the faculty of the architecture programme at the University of Toronto; since then, he has been active in architecture, urban design, and heritage preservation in Toronto and across Canada. He and his partners in Baird Sampson Neuert Architects have won five Canadian Architect Awards of Excellence (most recently in 2002), as well as a Governor General's Award for Architecture in 1995. In 1992, he won the Toronto Arts Foundation's Architecture and Design Award, and in 2000, he won the da Vinci Medal of the Ontario Association of Architects. He is the author and editor of numerous books, including *Meaning in Architecture* (with Charles Jencks) (1968); *Alvar Aalto* (1969); *The Space of Appearance* (1995); and *Queues, Rendezvous, Riots* (with Mark Lewis) (1995). From 1993 to 2004, he was a member of the faculty of the Graduate School of Design at Harvard University, where he served as G. Ware Travelstead Professor of Architecture, and Director of the M Arch I and M Arch II programmes. He retired from Harvard in 2004, and took up his current position as Dean of the Faculty of Architecture, Landscape and Design, University of Toronto in July of that year.

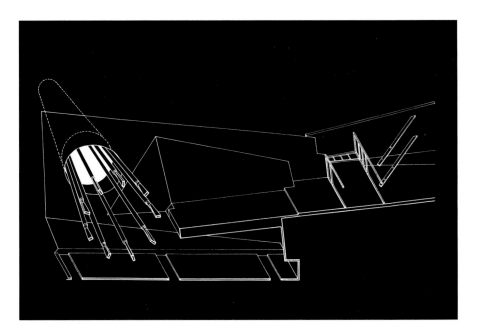

Peter Cardew, Stone Band School, Stone Indian Reserve No.1, Chilcotin

IDEAS OF CANADIAN ARCHITECTURE
Sherry McKay

Anyone with the slightest understanding of how cultures work knows that defining a culture, saying what it is for members of that culture, is always a major and, even in undemocratic societies, a democratic contest. There are canonical authorities to be selected and regularly revised, debated, reselected, or dismissed. There are ideas of good and evil, belonging or not belonging (the same and the different), hierarchies of value to be specified, discussed, rediscussed and settled or not.

—Edward Said

1. For a description of this problematic, see Gülsüm Baydar, "The Cultural Burden of Architecture," *Journal of Architectural Education*, vol. 57, no. 4 (May 2004), 19-27.

2. Alan Gowans, Preface to *Looking at Architecture in Canada* (1958), reprinted in *Building Canada: An Architectural History of Canadian Life* (Toronto: Oxford University Life, 1966), XVIII.

3. Ibid., XVII.

"The idea of Canadian architecture" is often nested in a number of concepts—culture, tradition, nationality—all of them problematically related to architecture.[1] Canadian architecture has not always had a continuous, official or representative history, as Alan Gowans pointed out in what was perhaps the first attempt to provide one in his 1958 book, *Looking at Architecture in Canada*. In its preface, he observes that in the history of Canadian architecture, in the absence of the "seminal," there is only "the commonplace, derivative and typical."[2] Consequently, Canadian architecture, being unfettered by "greatness or originality," is a more direct, uncomplicated expression "of all the great ideas, changing tastes, and permanent values of Western civilization."[3] Clearly, this is a misrepresentation, as an unviable idea of Canadian architecture then—despite the Cold War context of its construction—as it is today. Harold Kalman's more recent narrative of Canadian architecture, although more architecturally inclusive as the 1990s demanded, could still locate an originating idea of Canadian architecture in a mid-nineteenth century university building constructed in Western

University College, University
of Toronto

Civilization's High Victorian eclectic style. The "architectural schizophrenia" that the building conveyed through the "stylistic compromise" of bringing together references to Early English, Byzantium and Italian palazzo architecture in a single "hybrid" building was, Kalman mused, perhaps one of the earliest ideas of Canadian architecture, agreeing with a commentator from the period who suggested: "we may call it the Canadian style."[4] Neither the nineteenth century observer nor the late twentieth century historian elaborates on who "we" are; this lack of consensus on the definition of "we" is perhaps consistent with that compromised and hybrid form.[5] Therefore, although there have been attempts to articulate an idea of Canadian architecture—a definitive, essential encapsulation that might describe simultaneously both the architecture and the nation, that might provide it with ancestors and progeny—such a monolithic endeavour seems fraught, complicated and inevitably inadequate.[6]

Historically, any idea of Canadian architecture has been "Janus-faced": looking to pasts and futures, to politics and practices, to material evidence and discourse. Rather than singular and static, any idea of Canadian architecture has been, or must be, multiple and mobile, hybrid and strategic. The trope within the phrase "Canadian architecture" can also be a problematic one if it implies some necessary identification of one set of cultural practices of a place with any singular notion of the nation.[7] As Edward Said reminds us in the opening epigram, any definition of culture should be considered a contested practice, and those referring to culture should be wary of constructions of it: they are often predicated on a determined selection of authorities and authoritative texts.[8] Said, among many, demands that we do not take for granted the terms of our discourse or inquiry. For example, what do we mean to evoke by the word "Canadian," and what role does it play in defining, limiting or giving identity to architecture? Does "Canadian" imply a nation, a bounded geography, a shared culture, roots, an imposition, a right? And how might it, as a geography-based identity, find its place on the global freeway? Architecture does not escape instability of meaning either: it too is a contested entity. Is it a professional practice, a legislated determination, a cultural performance, an aesthetic judgement? As a way of coming to terms with this shifting of meaning and the unreliability of history—which contemporary theory demands we attend to—we need to discuss ideas of

4. Harold Kalman, speaking of University College, University of Toronto (1858), in *A Concise History of Canadian Architecture* (Oxford and Don Mills, Ont.: Oxford University Press, 2000), 250.

5. For a more extensive discussion of the ideological aspects of architectural history writing, see James Viloria, "The Politics of 'We' in the Construction of Collective Identities in Histories of Architecture in Canada," *Journal for the Society for the Study of Architecture in Canada*, vol. 24, no. 4 (1999), 10-17.

6. See Viloria for a discussion of Gowans, Kalman and *Documents in Canadian Architecture*, Geoffrey Simmins, ed. (Peterborough, Ont.: Broadview Press, 1992). More focused thematic histories could be added to Viloria's list, including Anthony Jackson's *The Democratization of Canadian Architecture* (Halifax, NS: Tech-Press, 1978) and *Space in Canadian Architecture* (Halifax, NS: Tech-Press, 1982).

7. See Homi K. Bhabha, "What is a nation," *Nation and Narration*, Ernst Renan, ed. (1882; reprint, London and New York: Routledge, 1990), 8-22. Interestingly, Renan's discussion of the nation as a contingent development of history rather than any essential characteristic—whether it be race, geography, or evolution of civilization—occurs just as a nationalist idea of architecture began to develop in Canada. See below.

8. Edward Said, "US: a disputed history of identity," *Le Monde* diplomatique (September 2004), 5.

9. Cited in Vikramaditya Prakash, "Identity Production in Postcolonial Indian Architecture: Re-Covering What We Never Had," *postcolonial space(s)*, G.B. Nalbantoglu and C.T. Wong, eds. (New York: Princeton Architectural Press, 1997), 39.

10. Melvin Charney, "Modern Movements in French-Canadian Architecture," *Process Architecture*, no. 5 (Tokyo: 1978), 15-26, and in Simmins, 268-280.

11. Eric Hobsbawn, *The Invention of Tradition* (Cambridge: Cambridge University Press, 1983), 1-14.

12. See Raymond Williams, *Culture and Society, 1780-1950* (London: Chatto and Windus, 1959 and New York: Columbia University Press, 1983) and *Keywords: A Vocabulary of Culture and Society*, 2d. ed. (London: Fontana, 1983). See also Alan O'Connor, "Keywords in Culture and Society," *Raymond Williams: Writing, Culture, Politics* (Oxford: Basil Blackwell, 1989), 49-67.

13. Said, 5.

14. Homi K. Bhabha, "DissemiNation: time, narrative, and the margins of the modern nation," *Nation and Narration*, Homi K. Bhabha, ed. (London and New York: Routledge, 1990), 292.

15. For a discussion of the terms "nation" and "nationalism," see Bill Ashcroft, Gareth Griffiths and Helen Tiffin, *Post-Colonial Studies: The Key Concepts* (London and New York: Routledge, 2000), 149-155.

16. Benedict Anderson, *Imagined Communities: Reflections on the Origin and Spread of Nationalism* (London and New York: Verso, 1991), 149-155.

17. Homi K. Bhabha, "Introduction: narrating the nation," *Nation and Narration*, Homi K. Bhabha, ed. (London and New York: Routledge, 1990), 1-7.

18. Ibid., 293. He goes on to quote Gellner that "The cultural shreds and patches used by nationalism are often arbitrary historical inventions. Any old shred would have served as well. But in no way does it follow that the principle of nationalism…is in the least contingent and accidental," 294.

Canadian architectures, a plurality that have possessed and dispossessed cultures and places. And if we understand Canadian architecture as a site of contestation, a construction, where identities are made and un-made, we should attend to its invention.

In perusing exhibition catalogues and books dedicated to the history of Canadian architecture, any singular idea of what it might be is elusive. It is not that history is bereft of such a discussion, but rather that the idea has altered over time as it has negotiated, for example, experience and the materiality of practice with theoretical knowledge, or institutional demands with typological inquiry. Robin Evans commented that: "Stories of origin are far more telling of their time of telling, than of the time they claim to tell."[9] This is also true of Melvin Charney, who in 1976, revealed an idea of Canadian architecture—modern, inventive, and "of the people"—in working class housing in Québec, where architectural criticism and history in the nineteenth and early twentieth centuries reported only debased and imperfect replications of some originating European model.[10] If these transferred, "essential" models could not produce a Canadian architecture, it was thought that other ideas, such as culture or tradition, might. However, culture and tradition are equally problematic notions, because it was thought in the nineteenth and into the twentieth century that these were in short supply in Canada. "Tradition," as Eric Hobsbawn has so famously stated, is an invention.[11] It does not form some bedrock upon which a national or cultural identity might be given secure footing. It cannot delimit or consolidate a transcendent nation. And because tradition proposes a stable or secure set of practices, it cannot authenticate a professional practice based on technological change, except through some form of policing. Likewise, as Raymond Williams has argued, what is meant by "culture" is relational and contextual. It is an activity, a process.[12] Consequently, any all-encompassing idea of Canadian architecture must be deferred: we are left with the recognition that such an identity rests upon historical interpretation.[13] Any such idea, then, is perhaps best considered a construct, a cultural process, and a social and textual affiliation.[14]

The idea of architecture is as profoundly unstable as are ideas of what is Canadian.[15] Both refer, as Benedict Anderson has theorized, to imagined communities.[16] Architecture, which has a role in portraying those communities, is also a complex strategy that can function in the name of or in resistance to the nation.[17] As Homi Bhabha has observed, "the historical necessity of the idea of the nation conflicts with contingent and arbitrary signs that signify the affective life of the national culture."[18] Therefore, to propose an "idea of Canadian architecture" is to, *importantly*, posit a constantly contested position, and I would like to suggest that blurred copies, trans-cultural production or non-conformities to known architectural styles or misquoted forms for example, might be, in fact, positive things.[19] Such ambiguity suggests that the "contingent and arbitrary signs that signify the affective life of the national culture" are still vital, and have not been overwhelmed or subsumed by some official definition—be it political or architectural—and might even open up new spaces for architectural conception.

The persistent suggestion that Canadian architecture manifested immature form or degraded style, so prevalent in the nineteenth but also in the twentieth century, was informed by the dynamics of British Imperialism. It was the expression of ethnographically influenced ideas of culture that sought to give value to art and culture according to ideas of progress and hence to a hierarchy that presumed a Western superiority. In that dynamic, Imperial centres, such as London, Paris or later Washington, established themselves as sources of knowledge for science, the arts and culture in general, while comparatively colonial settlements were found to be inferior. In the early twentieth century, "Arts and Crafts" theory turned architectural attention to vernacular practice and led to a conception of Canadian architecture as developing from long-embedded, localized techniques that adapted European traditions of how to deal with climate, geography and local materials. Such traditions, however, were simultaneously contradicted by the technological modernization occurring in the United States. Nationalist and cultural ideas of Canadian architecture did not always coincide with the professional idea of Canadian architecture: the former often looked to the Empire, the latter to the modernization south of the border.[20] So, while anti-American rhetoric might migrate between political text and architectural journalism in the interest of establishing differences, Canadian architects often traversed political boundaries in the interest of shared professional aspirations. The examples reveal that paradox and ambivalence accompanied cultural and architectural identity. The idea that Canadian architecture consisted in ornamented modern construction, as John Lyle proposed in the 1920s and 1930s, was contested by his contemporaries, who thought that ornament was irrelevant and form (determined by climate or materials) an anachronism given technological developments.[21] In the 1950s, West Coast architects asserted that architecture should be rooted in the landscape; the landscape to which they referred influenced the modern and abstract design of the whole Pacific Rim that could also be found internationally.

19. Contemporary post-colonial concepts of alterity, mimicry and hybridity provide other ways of thinking about empowered margins and cross-cultural production, ways that escape "reactionary nationalism" and an "introverted obsession with heritage." See Doreen Massey, "Power-geometry and a progressive sense of place," *Mapping the Futures: Local Cultures, Global Change*, Jon Bird, Barry Curtis, Tim Putnam, George Robertson and Lisa Tickner, eds. (London and New York: Routledge, 1993) 59-69. Quote is from page 63.

20. Angela Carr, "Indices of Identity: A Canadian Architectural Practice in the Second Half of the Nineteenth Century," *Society for the Study of Architecture in Canada Bulletin*, vol. 21, no.1 (March 1996), 11-17.

21. Ernest Cormier, for example, who stressed the constructive, rather than ornamental, aspect of architecture, believed regional and even national differences were fading and that standardization due to a scientific method would determine architecture. See Jean Chauvin, *Ateliers. Études sur vingt-deux peintres et sculpteurs canadiens* (New York and Montréal: Louis Carrier & Cie., 1928), 28-40, and in Simmins, 160-166; Ernest Cormier, "Architecture, Bâtiment," *Construction*, vol. 2, no. 10 (January 1947), 29-30, and in Simmins, 166-170.

22. Kelly Crossman, *Architecture in Transition: From Art to Practice*, 1885-1906 (Kingston, Ont. and Montréal: McGill-Queen's University Press, 1987), 129.

23. Charney in Simmins, 268-271.

24. Andrew Gruft, *A Measure of Consensus: Canadian Architecture in Transition* (Vancouver: University of British Columbia Fine Arts Gallery, 1986), 51.

25. See, for example, Gruft; and in Simmins see John Lyle, Ernest Cormier and The Massey Royal Commission.

26. Said, 5.

27. See, for example, Gowans and Jackson, *Space in Canadian*

Architecture. Jackson concludes his book: "It is only through this process of acknowledging and sublimating *our* realities, *our* myths and *our* dreams, that a Canadian architecture will emerge," 30.

28. Even when A.W.N. Pugin or Abbé Laugier, with their demand for a logical construction and emphasis on utility, are called upon to prove some admirable aspect of Canadian humble wooden buildings, it is with an eye to the European model that should be consulted. See the mid-century writings by William Hay, "The Late Mr. Pugin and the Revival of Christian Architecture," *Anglo American Magazine*, II (January-July 1853), 70-73, and "Architecture for the Meridian of Canada," *Anglo-American Magazine*, II (January-July 1853), 253-255, and commentary about Hay in Simmins, 43-58.

29. See particularly his frontispiece to the 1901 edition. For one of several discussions of Sir Banister, see Baydar.

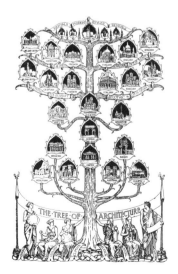

Tree of Architecture

The idea that Canadian architecture should be closely bonded to the nation state was prevalent in the early twentieth century,[22] but by the late 1970s it was suggested that it was rooted in resistance to the state;[23] a decade later, it was proposed that Canadian architecture entailed, with some qualification, an autonomous discipline.[24] Repeatedly through history, even recent history, Canadian architecture has been thought of as in "transition" or "emerging."[25] In other words, the idea of Canadian architecture has shifted with the times and in response to myriad circumstances. There is no transcendent Canada, or architecture, to which an idea of Canadian architecture can refer.

> The writing of history is the royal road to the definition of a country and that the identity of a society is in large part a function of historical interpretation, which is fraught with contested claims and counterclaims. [26]

Historical overviews of Canadian architecture suggest that from the eighteenth until well into the twentieth century, architectural designs and buildings were poor replications.[27] A survey of the documentary history of architecture in Canada would reveal a number of different ways in which Canadian architecture has been conceived that vary according to architectural theory and its conjunction with practice. The absence of a distinctively Canadian architecture, or the presence in its stead of an architecture that is misshapen or corrupted, imply the possibilities or prospects of another type of architecture. The criticism voiced in these texts confirms an official view of culture and history—that there are superior cultures elsewhere, centres from which a civilizing mission emanates to the peripheries and manages its evolution. These early ideas of Canadian architecture as peripheral to the architectural centres of Paris or London were the product of an Imperial discourse that manifested colonial sites, while they created the homeland: what it meant to be Paris or London, or even Edinburgh or Chicago. The power of the superior model and its "more authentic" origin worked to maintain the superiority of the centre over any peripheral production. According to this logic, any idea of Canadian architecture would necessarily respond to both inherited ideas of civilization and the exigencies of place.[28] That architecture was implicated in this construction of Imperial centres and colonial margins is manifestly demonstrated in Sir Banister Fletcher's *A History of Architecture on the Comparative Method*.[29] And it is clearly this logic that permeates much of the early commentary on Canadian architecture: including nineteenth century statements such as "…progress in architecture generally goes hand in hand with the blossoming of civilization and progress in science…[where] inhabitants must settle for public buildings and housing that are crude and devoid of decoration, we can only expect to find an uncouth and unrefined society. By making improvements to the buildings, we can follow quite accurately the progressive stages achieved by the community as it evolves…."[30] The idea that a "Canadian architecture" was lacking something essential persisted, despite architectural evidence to the contrary. It is a paradox worth examining. These same texts, while noting that the best architecture in Canada was but "a gradual approximation to a truer taste" found elsewhere, could also point to improvements in response to climate or materials that such a deviation provided.[31] Responses to the circumstances of climate, light, available materials or local resources intervened in the Imperial construction of meaning. By the mid-nineteenth century, the architectural theorizing of the Gothic Revival would make these professional enthusiasms more than merely the necessity of new terrains and limited means.[32]

Immediately following Confederation in 1867, Gothic Revival sentiments served to ratify Lord Dufferin's picturesque medievalist embellishment of Québec City, which sought to solidify mythic bonds between Scotland and Québec based on their shared harsh climate, proposing ties to Old Scotland as more prominent than those to Old France and countering Québec shopkeepers who preferred a modern, not a "national" city.[33] Climate, geography and topography (and the picturesque aesthetic prevalent at the time) were a highly self-conscious effort directed toward identity-creation. All in the interest of strengthening unity at a time of a fractious regional contingency, as well as a competing Empire to the south and the demobilizing of British troops. Hence, the idea of Canadian architecture resides in the specificity of time and place.[34]

According to Kelly Crossman, the idea of an explicitly Canadian, national, architecture was promoted in the first decade of the twentieth century, when "the idea that architecture should be expressive of history, climate and national life had taken hold in Canada."[35] Crossman shows that the very explicit expression of a nationalist idea of Canadian architecture that occurred at that time was a complex and determined endeavour initiated by a group of prominent architects. That it developed some years after Confederation intimates that it was not a direct response to political nation building; that it arose during the expansion of the dominion suggests that it was not irrelevant either. At the same time, as architecture was to be expressive of history, it was also envisioned that "[t]he stamp of originality which we hope will be placed on our buildings may prove that Canada is a nation…."[36] This new appraisal of architecture relied on the migration of ideas originating outside the halls of Canadian political power and indeed beyond the geographical boundaries of the new nation. The nationalist idea drew

30. Luc Noppen, "The British Contribution to the Architectural Identity of Old Québec," *Society for the Study of Architecture in Canada Bulletin*, vol. 21, no.1 (March 1996), 4-10. Quote is on page 6 and is from an 1805 speech recorded in Pierre-Georges Roy, "L'Hôtel Union ou Saint-Georges à Québec," *Bulletin des recherches historiques*, vol. 43, no. 1 (1937), 3-17.

31. See, for example, James Beaven, "Recreations of a Long Vacation; or, "A Visit to Indian Missions in Upper Canada" (1846), 185-196, excerpted in Simmins, 26-32.

32. The Gothic Revival in Europe was also imbricated with nationalist thinking. For example, Viollet-le-Duc in France attributed national characteristics to the Gothic, as did Augustus Welby Pugin in England. See Peter Collins, "Gothic Nationalism," *Changing Ideals in Modern Architecture*, 1750-1950 (London: Faber & Faber and Montréal: McGill University Press, 1965), 100-105. See also Crossman, 109-121. Also associated with the Gothic Revival was the idea that Canadian architecture was a northern style, responding to climate and materials.

33. Georges Drolet, "The Mighty Empire of the Past: Lord Dufferin's 1875 Embellishment Proposals for Québec City," *Society for the Study of Architecture in Canada Bulletin*, vol. 21, no. 1 (March 1996), 18-24.

34. At the same time, the mythologized connection between Scotland and Québec served to naturalize the Scottish presence and Canada's place within the Empire for some time to come. Hence, Isabelle Gournay could claim that: "Scottish implant was facilitated by the physical and cultural kinship between Scotland and Québec, and by their equally harsh climates, comparable desires of political and cultural individuation within the British Empire, and awareness of powerful neighbours south of their borders whose domination they feared. It was eased by the presence of an influential Scottish business community in Montréal and by the long tradition of intellectual kinship between France and Scotland." Isabelle

Gournay, "The First Leaders of McGill's School of Architecture: Stewart Henbest Capper, Percy Nobbs, and Ramsay Traquair," *Society for the Study of Architecture in Canada Bulletin*, vol. 21, no. 3 (September 1996), 66, n. 27.

35. Crossman, 109.

36. Ibid., 109.

37. Ibid., 145.

38. Nobbs is talking about the exemplary work of Norman Shaw in 1907, in Crossman, 134.

39. Crossman, 145.

40. Ibid., 145.

41. The Premier of Saskatchewan looked to the Minnesota state capitol as an exemplary precedent for the new Legislature Building in Regina. See Crossman, 143-144.

42. Percy Nobbs, "The English Tradition in Canada," *Architectural Review* 55 (June 1924), 238. Quoted in Gournay, 64.

43. Percy Nobbs, "Architecture in Canada" (London: Royal Institute of British Architects, 1924), 9, 11. Quoted in Gournay, 64.

44. Eric Arthur, "Architecture," *The Royal Commission on National Development in the Arts, Letters, and Sciences* (Ottawa: 1951) n.p..

its inspiration from theoretical developments in Great Britain, the "Arts and Crafts" movement generally and its Scottish incarnation specifically. It consequently privileged an appreciation for the crafting of local materials, indigenous decorative motifs, practicality of form and detail, and their basis in construction. It also cultivated sensitivity to vernacular practices as a source of knowledge for contemporary practice and an understanding of architecture as an outgrowth of a way of life.

This idea of a nationalist architecture was articulated through "Arts and Crafts" theory, which was transformed in the Canadian context to resolve issues of practice encountered there, and to encourage the development of architecture in a cultural context having "more vernacular than canonical buildings."[37] However, Percy Nobbs, a prominent spokesman of the nationalist idea of Canadian architecture and "Arts and Crafts" theory, associated the general principles afforded by the latter with a specific culture and tradition—the "natural and rightful heritage" of Great Britain and France. For public buildings, he advocated "Englishness—severe, masculine, refined," a freer kind of classicism.[38] Nobbs intended to distinguish Canadian public buildings from American and their Beaux-Arts Academic style, which he dismissed as "thoroughly non-British in feeling."[39] In contrast, "the modern Free Classic evolved for English Public Buildings, and sometimes called the Anglo-Classic or Imperial Style" was recommended for its distinctive national character.[40] Nevertheless, American accomplishment in both building technology and Beaux Arts planning were clearly evident in Canadian architecture, and western politicians, among others, viewed American models favourably.[41] Eventually, by the mid-1920s, Nobbs would have to concede that: "far more cultural unity (outside the realm of political ideals) exists between Canada and the United States, than between Canada and England. It is probably of far greater significance to us…that the country is situated on the North American continent, than [the fact] that it is within the hegemony of the British Empire."[42] In the same year, he concluded "'beyond the practicality and roof making' Canadian architecture was still 'a polite fiction. It was too American to British eyes and too British to American.'"[43]

If the nation (qualified by climate and materials, and directed by the knowledge of the vernacular) was to be the underpinning of a Canadian architecture in the early decades of the twentieth century, then the region was a more convincing idea by mid-century. Although the Massey Commission of 1949-1951 emphasized the national role of regional architecture—as one of its authors, Eric Arthur, noted: "To talk of a Canadian architecture is not far-fetched—so long as one recognizes differences….To talk, on the other hand, of a Canadian architecture indistinguishable in manner from coast to coast is to deny the basic principles of modern architecture and to ignore the cultural heritage of our country."[44] One such recognized difference was the mythic West Coast style—a regional expression comprised of local material and construction ingenuity, openness to the extra-territorial Pacific Rim, a transformed idea of a northern country and the technical aesthetic of modern Californian architecture.[45] As Northrop Frye cautioned in *The Bush Garden*, twenty years later, "the question of Canadian identity, so far as it affects the creative imagination, is not a 'Canadian' question at all, but a regional question."[46] And in distinguishing "Canadian unity and identity," he argues: "identity is local and regional, rooted in the imagination and in the work of culture; unity is national in reference, international in perspective and rooted in a political feeling."[47] Frye's desire to open up a space between unity and identity, meant opening up a space between nationalism and culture. It intimates an artifice in the constructing of both—a contingency.

What do these theoretical and historical discourses mean to the works exhibited here? First of all, they suggest that as a practice that negotiates national narratives and translates cultural expectations, the work might—perhaps must—contain counter-narratives (of different histories, cultures and attitudes to resources, for example) that erase, as they evoke, any totalizing boundaries or ambitions of the nation. They might—perhaps must—disturb the ideological manoeuvres through which imagined communities are given essentialist or transcendent identities. Architecture, in its material presence and circumstantial nature, in calling up imagined communities, might also imagine communities differently.

The hybridity that caused such anxiety in the nineteenth century might suggest more hopeful things when applied to contemporary work, as in projects that reference both First Nations and canonized Western tradition, as exemplified in Busby + Associates' Nicola Valley Institute of Technology or Peter Cardew's Stone Band School—the latter built under the auspices of the Stone Band Council, Stone Indian Reserve No.1 and Public Works Canada. Both projects sought to evoke traditions embedded in the patterns of building that were significant in the landscape and with their respective clients. Here, the hybrid marks less a site of unease, as it did in the past when purity of cultural reference was preferred, than it does a point of constant being "otherwise."

One of the recurring conceptions of Canadian architecture is that it is concerned with nature—climate, topography, landscape and, more recently, ecology. But as the shifts in cognates, the terms associating buildings with nature, suggest, the relationship between architecture and landscape is a negotiated position. Contemporary theory proposes that enduring ideas, traditions,

45. On the "West Coast Style," see Sherry McKay, "Western Homes, Western Living," *Society for the Study of Architecture in Canada Bulletin*, vol. I, no. 3 (September 1989), 65-75; on the continuation of ideas about Canada's northern climate see Arthur Erickson, *The Architecture of Arthur Erickson* (Montréal: Tundra Books, 1973), 33. For the influence of Californian architects see McKay; and for a discussion of how regionalism negotiated modernism, including the Californian architects see Rhodri Windsor-Liscombe, *The New Spirit: Modern Architecture in Vancouver, 1938-1963* (Montréal: Centre Canadien d'architecture/Canadian Centre for Architecture and Vancouver: Douglas & McIntyre, 1997).

46. Northrop Frye, Preface, *The Bush Garden: Essays on the Canadian Imagination* (Toronto: Anansi Press, 1971), i.

47. Ibid., ii.

48. George Thomas Kapelos, *Interpretations of Nature: Contemporary Canadian Architecture, Landscape and Urbanism* (Kleinburg, Ont.: McMichael Canadian Art Collection, 1994), 57.

49. For a concise outline of this argument, see John McMinn and Marco Polo, "Regional Responses to Sustainable Architecture in Canada: Two Case Studies," paper given at the ACSA Regional Conference, Vancouver, October 14-17, 2004. The two case studies discussed are Nicola Valley Institute of Technology, Merritt, British Columbia, by Busby + Associates Architects, and Jackson-Triggs Estate Winery, Niagara-on-the-Lake, Ontario, by KPMB Architects.

50. Dean Hawkes, Jane McDonald and Koen Steemers, *The Selective Environment: An Approach to Environmentally Responsive Architecture* (London and New York: Spon Press, 2002), 85-90. Quote is from page 85. The commentary is not without its own myths of "the cold Canadian winter."

51. Ibid., 90.

52. See the discussion by Peter Pran, Herbert Enns, Beth Kapusta and Kim Storey in "The Canadian Architect 1994 Awards of Excellence," *Canadian Architect* (December 1994), 17-21.

53. Christopher Macdonald, "Eloquent Resistance," *Canadian Architect* (May 1997), 16-23. Macdonald mentions the work of Benisch and the heritage of Hans Scharoun, 20.

54. Jim Taggart, "Patkau Architects," *Interdisciplinary Architecture*, Nicoletta Trasi, ed. (Chichester: Wiley-Academy, 2001), 191-195. Quotes are from page 195.

55. Macdonald, 20, 22.

56. Trevor Boddy, "Rain Coast Culture," *Architecture*, vol. 84, no. 9 (September 1995), 66-73. Quote is from page 66.

57. George Wagner, "Critique: Keeping Secrets," *Canadian Architect*, vol. 40, no. 11 (November 1995), 22-27. Quote is from page 25.

Busby + Associates, Nicola Valley Institute of Technology, Merritt, BC

are processes; they are constructed, and as such can be dismantled, displaced, conserved or renovated. While it may be true that "in Canada…myths of nature are pervasive, deeply rooted, and all powerful,"[48] those myths are multiple, often conciliatory, at times contesting, and occasionally assuming new conjugations. A renegotiation of those myths of nature can be seen in contemporary discourses about sustainability, where a regional dimension, based on "vernacular practices" wrought from material responses to climate, geological conditions and local labour, among other things, is proposed to imbue scientifically derived criteria for sustainability with the qualitative apprehension of culture.[49] Such a balance between a global discourse and a local myth is evident in the Strawberry Vale Elementary School by Patkau Architects. For an international audience, Strawberry Vale exists within a tradition of low-energy school design that began with a school in England and extends across northern latitudes.[50] Here, "the understanding of environmental processes now allows a more refined response to the nature of the environment."[51] For an immediate constituency, Strawberry Vale recalls a regionally inflected engagement with topography, local interests and material culture. While not dismissing the environmental strategies with which the building is endowed,[52] or its position within a different northern European tradition,[53] commentators in the national press highlight the figuring of the environment as landscape. It is evoked by *circulation* where a "meandering spine is a figurative extension of the forest paths outside" and *form* "symbolic of the surrounding landscape."[54] References to the landscape as both nature and artifice are understood in the building plan and section that shifts in response to the terrain. It is "the thematic regard for landscape," be it circulation, visual access, or "rooms as spatial landscapes" that strikes a chord with local reviewers.[55] Conversely, Peter Cardew's Belkin Art Gallery calls up the landscape differently. Its interiors are less reverent to spectacular distant views and more accommodating of local light and nature seen obliquely. While this might seem, however tangentially, to place the building in an indigenous landscape tradition, resident critics have interpreted nature as architecture's undoing, a "false authority"[56] or stemming from "views which seem always to advance sentimental and often patronizing mythologies while denying the limits, conventions, and immediacy of the surrounding context."[57] Ideas of Canadian architecture thus differ according to context and the discourses that seek to position it. While, at one time, the "Janus-face" of Canadian architecture looked to the Imperial centre and the contingencies of material and labour, it now looks to the global freeway and the particularities of the context.

A view to the global freeway and the particularities of context is evident in the work of Kuwabara Payne McKenna Blumberg (KPMB). Materials chosen for their thematic contribution rather than their place of origin, and forms derived from distant sources and typological abstractions, locate buildings within existing urban contexts. Aluminum and steel are understood as surface and texture rather than as references to local materials; the typological forms of rotunda, tower, square and colonnade respond to the local norms of site. The play between convention and invention, the tactile qualities of materials and the unsure spatial perceptions they evoke, defines a new kind of hybrid architecture.[58]

A clearly visible duality has also been noted in the work of Saucier + Perrotte. There is a certain vacillation in the discussion of the work, locating it within a particular cultural provenance, French Canada, but also elsewhere, in a "different vocabulary."[59] As Kurt Forster concludes, their work is "clearly rooted in the context of a distinctive regional culture," yet "their work increasingly shows the influence of other references and registers difference."[60] Others have identified "unorthodox qualities [that] suggest a link with recent European rather than North American examples."[61] And while natural landscape as a "fundamental part of the Canadian psyche"[62] can still be referenced in their Canadian Embassy project for Berlin or "the typology of traditional Québécoise rural dwellings" in a villa that displays a complex relationship with the landscape,[63] it is the idea of Canadian architecture suggested in their Cinématèque Québécoise that is interesting. Here, any reference to an essential Canadian psyche is replaced by an architecture that "highlights the ambiguous relationships between image, viewer and viewed,"[64] and hence the making and unmaking of meaning, the illusive and illusionary construction of identity.

The contemporary architecture on view in this exhibition displays a range of responses to conventions of built form and regional expression ranging from decorous acknowledgement to civil disagreement. It is difficult to detect any essences underlying responses to context, be it landscape, urban fabric or historical form. Uncanny villas, uncustomary additions to existing building complexes and architecture that calls up two or more traditions simultaneously and without implied hierarchies, evoke counter-narratives. Ecological and sustainable agendas demand both global vision and local knowledge. Insight derived from cinema, video and digitally modeled environments suggests that identity is mutable, re-formed by context and time. Allusive forms and illusive spaces are apt responses to present circumstances of migration and global flows, which place new demands on identity claims and boundary making. The insertion of a library in a

58. *Kuwabara Payne McKenna Blumberg*, Foreword by George Baird, Introduction by Detlef Mertins (Gloucester, MA: Rockport Publishers, 1998).

59. Essy Baniassad, Preface, *Saucier + Perrotte Architectes, 1995-2002*, Brian Carter, ed. (Halifax: TUNS Press, 2004), 11.

60. Brian Carter, "Absence/ separation/ difference," *Saucier + Perrotte Architectes, 1995-2002*, Brian Carter, ed. (Halifax: TUNS Press, 2004), 17.

61. Kurt W. Forster, "Miracle in Montréal," *Canadian Architect* 45 (August 2000), 20-25. Quote is from page 23.

62. Carter, 15.

63. Beth Kapusta, "The Dynamics of an Ideal Villa," *Canadian Architect* 41 (February 1996), 16-21. Quote is from page 19.

64. Carter, 14.

Saucier + Perrotte architectes, Collège Gérald-Godin, Montréal former chapel (Saucier + Perrotte's Collège Gérald-Godin), the tracing of biodiversity over an established landscape mythology (Patkau Architects' Strawberry Vale Elementary School), or the mimicking of formal conventions (KPMB's Kitchener City Hall) are "the contingent and arbitrary signs that signify the affective life of the national culture," of which Bhabha spoke. Hence, the works exhibited here suggest palimpsests rather than originating essences and might be where one looks for ideas of Canadian architecture.

FIGURES

p.190 Peter Cardew Architects, Stone Band School, Stone Indian Reserve No.1, Chilcotin, 1992.

p.192 University College, University of Toronto, Toronto, Ontario, 1856-1859.

Photograph c. 1859, NAC/C-21670.

p. 195 The Tree of Architecture: Sir Banister Fletcher, *A History of Architecture on the Comparative Method for the Student, Craftsman and Amateur*, 16th ed. (1901; reprint, London: B.T. Batsford Ltd., 1954), frontispiece.

p. 199 Nicola Valley Institute of Technology, Merritt, BC.

p. 200 Saucier + Perrotte architectes, Collège Gérald-Godin, Montréal, 1999.

SHERRY McKAY is Associate Professor of Architectural History and Theory at the School of Architecture, University of British Columbia, Vancouver. Her publications include "Urban Housekeeping" and "Keeping the House Modern," *BC Studies* (2004); "Dream Homes," *Dream Home, Work by René van Halm* (2002); "Architectural Negotiations of the Pacific Rim," *Bulletin de l'Institute Pierre Renouvin* (2000); "Unveiled Borders: Le Corbusier and Algiers in the 1930s," *L'Image* (2000); "'Mediterraneanism': The Politics of Architectural Production in Algiers," *City and Society* (2000); *Cultural Continuity, Technological Transformation: KST, a case study.* (exhibition and catalogue: Vancouver 2000); and *Assembling Utopia: Packaging the Home* (exhibition and catalogue: Vancouver 1999, Tokyo 2000). McKay is co-editor of *Disciplining Bodies in the Gymnasium: Memory, Monument, Modernism* (Routledge, 2004).

Dan Hanganu,
Pointe-à-Callière museum,
Montréal

CONTEMPORARY ARCHITECTURE IN QUÉBEC: *LA DIFFERENCE*
Georges Adamczyk

1. The six firms whose projects and accomplishments are presented here have participated in nearly thirty-five architectural competitions since 1991. See *Leap* web site: http//www.leap.umontreal.ca

When Dan Hanganu took his place as a first-class architect on both local and international levels, most of the Québec architects presented in this exhibition were only just obtaining their diplomas and making their professional debuts. This new generation that emerged in the 1980s enthusiastically undertook an architectural revival not only in Québec, but in Canada as well. Radical or reasonable, experimentalist or efficient, eloquently or silently, they tackled what we call "the architectural competition years"[1] without any kind of manifesto. This situation was supported by numerous factors: initiatives by the ministère de la Culture et des Communications du Québec, programmes from the Canada Council for the Arts, the *ARQ: Architecture/Québec* competitions, the last of Alcan's Lecture Series, the opening of the Canadian Centre for Architecture in Montréal, and finally, but most importantly, the desire of these architects to move away from the models handed down to them since the 1960s.

As we analyse the projects of the architects who have marked the past ten years, we discover the particular concerns that emerged with each commission, as well as original narratives, distinct attitudes, and diverse influences. It is the difference of expression that characterizes these architects and their ideas. Should this "difference" be attributed to the competitions that encouraged participants to express their individuality at the expense of sharing with or drawing from a common architectural design culture? Or perhaps this rebellious process is what enhances the culture surrounding architectural design? If so, perhaps weaving together the many historical and cultural threads will provide a better understanding of this situation.

THE STATE OF PLACES: FROM NEW FRANCE TO QUÉBEC

The perception or interpretation of contemporary architecture in Québec changes according to the point of view we adopt. If viewed from the West Coast of Canada, for example, we might celebrate what makes Québec architecture different and view the distinction as a contribution to a rich and diverse national culture; whereas, if seen from Paris, we might be perplexed by the resistance to American pragmatism. The influence of the past may be fading away, while the future is more uncertain everyday. The main building at the University of Montréal, designed by Ernest Cormier in the late 1920s, is without a doubt the last great architectural accomplishment that marks the French spirit in Québec. It towers over a culture in which identity and diversity are intertwined. This paradox gave birth to a new "material ecstasy."[2]

2. See *Extase matérielle* by J.M.G. Le Clézio (Paris: Gallimard, 1967), n.p..

In 1949, two works appeared that would determine the coming of artistic modernity to Québec: Paul-Émile Borduas and his colleagues signed *Refus Global*, and Gérard Morisset published *L'architecture en Nouvelle-France*. The "Revolution tranquille" of the 1960s reached its apogee in 1967, with the World Expo in Montréal. Since then, Québec has oscillated between the symbolic construction of collective and singular memory and the political accomplishment of a multicultural society. When combined, these two conflicting attitudes mix the desire to withdraw into local familiarity and the struggle against all forms of provincialism. It is therefore not particularly shocking to discover in Montréal a built landscape where signs of tradition and the most forceful emblems of the international style mix freely.

It is even less surprising, leaving Montréal to follow the Saint Lawrence River towards Québec City, to discover another world where this "dislocation" between culture and building takes on its meaning as we try to grasp the connection between the imagination and reality of the land.[3] In this region, architecture does not have the authority or power to domesticate the extent of the territory, and therefore its ability to create the illusion of order and finitude. If this is true for the entire urbanized world, it is even more crucial in Québec, since the apparent order of a spatial structure punctuated with the spires of religious buildings conceals a different present-day reality. Melvin Charney, a great master of paradox, describes the situation in his 1971 essay, "Pour une définition de l'architecture au Québec." Contrary to Claude Beaulieu's thesis that limits an interpretation of Canadian architecture to the formal and foreign inspired elements of buildings,[4] Melvin Charney proposes that we think about architecture in terms of relationships. He suggests that we locate in new architecture what makes the ordinary

3. See Benoît Goetz, *La dislocation: Architecture et philosophie* (Paris: Les Éditions de la passion, 2001), n.p..

4. Claude Beaulieu, *L'architecture contemporaine au Canada français* (Québec: Ministère des affaires culturelles, 1969), n.p..

devices of these buildings vital and popular. He ends the essay with a discussion of the divisive debate over belonging to New France or French Canada:

> In Québec, like elsewhere, valid architecture challenges the state of architecture itself. We cannot find answers in the usual places. Inevitably, the social condition of the individual as an architect is emphasized. This means that the liberation of the architect depends on the political and social liberation of the individual and of the community. It also depends on the expression of a renewed and original Québécois identity. Unfortunately, the cultural hegemony of traditional architecture continues still. But now, at least, it is more and more an anachronism.[5]

Here, the influential Catholic philosopher, Jacques Maritain's theme of "the responsibility of the artist" is reformulated in secular terms.[6] It is no longer a question of personal conscience and the transcendental idea of art, but rather the artist's commitment and role as the creator of a symbolic and authentic world within popular culture.

THE RETURN OF ARCHITECTURE

In the 1980s, a resistance grew toward the dominant idea of functionalism. This crisis was characterized by a return to tradition combined with a re-evaluation of modernism, and a rediscovery of the urban physical space as an architectural form of social space. The resultant "awakening of architecture" appeared as the public showed a growing interest in built heritage and places of memory, and the aesthetic crisis in modern architecture that resulted was resolved with a "postmodern" attitude. It was this cultural ground that the various architectural trends in Québec shared, but not without certain tensions. Historical areas that had previously interested only antique dealers and historians from l'Île d'Orléans to Montréal's Saint-Jean-Baptiste quarter became the very cause of the regionalist revival and the "reappropriation" of constructed culture. This connection between old and new permeated developments in urban art and architecture demonstrating the "reconquest" of the territory: Montréal's Alcan House (1981-1983), designed by ARCOP (Architects in Co-partnership); the *Musée de la civilisation* in Québec City (1987), designed by Moshe Safdie just two years after the old city was included on UNESCO's World Heritage List; the Centre Canadien d'architecture/Canadian Centre for Architecture (1989), designed by Peter Rose and Phyllis Lambert; and the development of Montréal's Old Port (1992) by architects and urban planners, Groupe Cardinal Hardy, in collaboration with Peter Rose. To various degrees these projects laid the groundwork for a new urbanity founded

5. Melvin Charney, "Pour une définition de l'architecture au Québec," *Architecture et urbanisme au Québec* (Montréal : Les Presses de l'Université de Montréal, 1971), 42.

6. Jacques Maritain, *La responsabilité de l'artiste* (Paris: ArthèmeFayard, 1961), n.p..

on respect for what was already there, for existing uses and customs, and for the built heritage. As a result, the idea of anachronism was challenged. These accomplishments changed the long-standing recognition and existing importance of the spatial and temporal presence of a reconquered past in order to open up to the major changes to come.

In this creative stance, the bricklayer and carpenter were just as meritorious as the architect, and a new generation of creators turned to local invention without conceding to cultural globalization. Jacques Rousseau (Maison Coloniale, 1990), Dan Hanganu in collaboration with Provencher Roy (Pointe-à-Callière museum, 1992), Louis-Paul Lemieux and the Atelier Kaos ("Immeuble boulevard" in Drummondville, 1992), Éric Gauthier from the firm Blouin, Faucher, Aubertin, Brodeur, Gauthier (Théâtre Espace Go, 1994), Saucier + Perrotte (Cinémathèque Québécoise, 1997), Pierre Thibault (Théâtre de la Dame de Cœur, 1995), Boutros and Pratte (Plaza Laurier, 1994), atelier big city (Parc de l'aventure basque en Amérique, 1996), and Saïa and Barbarese (Centre sportif de la Petite-Bourgogne, 1998) are some of the architects who contributed to defining a new *architecture québécoise*. We must remember, however, that these were exceptional cases and we must not forget the daily difficulties architects experience in getting their contributions to culture recognized.

Having briefly situated the architectural scene, it would be tempting to see it as nothing but the normal result of prevailing cultural and social conditions. However, this would underestimate the intellectual and professional challenges that the aesthetic question poses in architecture. Indeed, just as in other fields of artistic creation, like contemporary art, architecture came to question its *raison d'être* and future.

THE DEBATE IN *ARQ*

In Québec, this debate was the central issue informing articles published regularly in the periodical, *ARQ: Architecture/Québec*, founded in the 1980s by three architects (Pierre Boyer-Mercier, Pierre Beaupré and Jean-Louis Robillard) with support from the Ordre des architectes du Québec. Today, *ARQ* is independent, and after the departure of his associates, Pierre Boyer-Mercier publishes the only cultural periodical dedicated to architecture in Québec. *ARQ*, and other publications of the 1980s were highly influential in bringing 1970s ideas about architecture in Québec to an end. Combined with the publication of *Livre blanc de l'architecture au*

cover, *ARQ 64*

Saucier + Perrotte, Cinémathèque Québécoise, Montréal

Québec in 1983 (edited by Patrick Blouin, then-president of the Ordre), we witnessed the founding of a lively architectural print culture in Québec. Small architectural reviews started to appear, such as *5th Column*, created by students of the School of Architecture at McGill University, and *Silo*, led by professors in the Department of Design at the Université du Québec à Montréal (UQAM). The Faculty of Environmental Design at the University of Montréal launched the multi-disciplinary journal, *Trames*. Odile Hénault, an architecture critic active in promoting a new generation of architects, founded the bilingual magazine, *Section A*, which during its two year existence brought an international dimension to the local debate. In these publications, eminent academics and architects known for their critical thought—George Baird, Henri Ciriani, Jean-Louis Cohen, Christian Devillers, Kenneth Frampton, Vittorio Gregotti, Joseph Paul Kleihues, and Álvaro Siza—brought an outsider's point of view to the local debates on public space and re-evaluations of modernism. Previously, the architectural discourse was almost exclusively the result of the research and cultural activities of Phyllis Lambert and the writings of Melvin Charney and Jean-Claude Marsan. Several works established the foundations of this new critical reflection. Of particular note are *Montréal, une esquisse du futur* by Jean-Claude Marsan (1983), *Architectures au xxe siècle au Québec* by Claude Bergeron (1989), *Ville Métaphore*, edited by Iréna Latek (1992), and *Architecture, forme urbaine et identité collective*, by Luc Noppen (1995).

ARQ fostered an inter-university movement of criticism. In addition to Beaupré, Boyer-Mercier and Robillard, new figures emerged from the teaching corps in theory and architectural history: Pierre-Richard Bisson, Denis Bilodeau, Yves Deschamps, Jacques Lachapelle (Université de Montréal); Ricardo Castro, Alberto Pérez-Gómez (McGill University); Claude Bergeron, Marc Grignon, Luc Noppen, Lucie K. Morisset (Université Laval); and François Giraldeau, France Vanlaethem and myself (UQAM). We were quickly joined by young practitioners and researchers such as Jean-François Bédard, Jean-Pierre Chupin, Anne Cormier, Éric Gauthier, Philippe Lupien and Louis Martin. Paul Faucher, a long-time associate of the review's founders, reflected on cultural issues in architecture and on the responsibility of architects. Four themes preoccupied these authors: cultural identity, the history of contemporary architecture, professional practice and the politics of architecture.

A special issue of *ARQ* titled, *L'architecture au Québec, les années 80*, which appeared in 1989, can be considered an overview of this period. The articles are organized in sections that reflect the sociology of the profession: building production; the debate on education and research; the architect's practice; the client-patron. The aesthetic question is not addressed directly, though it punctuates each section with observations that are sometimes severe and other times optimistic. France Vanlaethem, who for several years directed ARQ's editorial committee before devoting herself to DoCoMoMo (Documentation and Conservation of Buildings, Sites and Neighbourhoods of the Modern Movement), brought the review's ideological programme back to the heritage of modern architecture in Québec.

Although at its foundation ARQ sought to lead architectural practice away from the influence of the international style by way of a radical stance inspired by Melvin Charney, the editors tended to promote a resistance to the arrival of "postmodernism." A "revised modernist perspective" was proposed as a substitute for the eclectic and populist practice that emerged as a way of compensating for the loss of skills in a context of cultural mutations. Trapped in an identity-focused argument, ARQ also had a negative effect—it did not comment on or criticize the new directions of architecture influenced by the philosophical and conceptual possibilities introduced by communications technologies. Thus, few writings can be found in ARQ that examine the trends of either "Supermodernism" or "Deconstructivism."

AESTHETICS AND POLITICS

To better grasp the conflict of interpretations that the term postmodernism suggests and the aesthetic and identity issues that it provoked in Québec during the last decade, we might refer to the French philosopher, Luc Ferry, who identifies three trends: postmodernism as exaggerated modernism; postmodernism as "revival" or "return" to tradition against modernism; and postmodernism as an overtaking of modernism. Ferry suggests that this last trend risks overtaking reason itself and, most critically, could promote an exhaustion of Western art and culture.[7] But is there another possible solution for contemporary architecture? Michael Freitag asks:

7. Luc Ferry, *Le sens du beau* (Paris: Livre de poche, 2001), 282-296.

> What can architects do? In exercising their profession, can they still attempt to express a symbolic meaning of social life, create a place of exchange and synthesis where the social fits its spirit and the tensions that worry it, its permanence and change into the world? And in which can the exterior world find itself humanly transfigured?[8]

8. Michel Freitag, *Architecture et société* (Paris: Éditions St-Martin, 1982), 87.

The aesthetic, by "its immediately cognitive and normative reach," must lead us to rediscover beauty—an aesthetic competence which, through movements and

9. Jacques Lachapelle, "Points de repère pour une histoire de la pratique," ARQ 40 (1987), 8-11.

styles like the "Arts and Crafts," Neoclassicism, Beaux Arts, *Art sacré* or Modernism, architects have demonstrated throughout time. But what has the architect become today? Jacques Lachapelle suggests that the rise of professionalism in the second half of the last century fostered the legitimacy of the architect's technical and economic expertise, while contributing to architecture's loss of artistic and cultural credibility.[9]

In his work, *Montréal en évolution*, Jean-Claude Marsan begins the history of Montréal with a section titled, "Au carrefour des circulations" (At the Crossroads of Circulations). It is a geographical evocation situating not only the physical place, but also the circumstances of a new civilization's emergence. In the latest edition, the book concludes with a new chapter titled, "Les méandres de l'architecture" (The Meanderings of Architecture).[10] The author recognizes the difficulties and obstacles imposed on a profession regulated by interests that irremediably exclude any debate on culture. If "the years of reappropriation" put an end to architectural utopias and real estate developer excesses, fostering public debate and the role of the citizen, they did not define an aesthetic perspective for architecture. As the Catalan architect and theorist, Ignasi de Solà-Morales, wrote:

10. Jean-Claude Marsan, *Montréal en évolution: historique du développement de l'architecture et de l'environnement urbain montréalais* (Laval: Éditions du Méridien, 1994), n.p..

> …the difference between the present situation and that of the academic culture unique to modern orthodoxy is that it is no longer possible today to formulate an aesthetic system that would be valid enough to be applicable above and beyond all circumstances that put it in motion.[11]

Influenced by the philosopher, Gianni Vattimo, Solà-Morales sees the architectural project as an intervention in a concrete reality open to interpretation. The situation and the object always determine the designer's approach. Interpretation can no longer be done in the name of historical truth and even less in the name of instrumental reason; it must also create "analogies" with existing matter, in order to elaborate the matter that gives the new construction its meaning. Inspired by post-Marxist thought identified as "weak thought," this attitude makes the "moment of the project" seem like a "moment of freedom," a strong and decisive instant. The idea promoted here is that design cannot be limited to the doctrine of history, nor to the search for a style. The architectural project is thought out in the making.

11. Ignasi de Solà-Morales, "From Contrast to Analogy: Theorizing a New Agenda for Architecture Theory" in *Theorizing a New Agenda for Architecture: An Anthology of Architectural Theory, 1965-1995*, Kate Nesbitt, ed. (New York: Princeton Architecture Press, 1996), 230-237.

Solà-Morales suggests that analogy is central to the architect's conceptual process. It is also a discursive strategy that gives order to dogmas and doctrines, and is firmly opposed to the theory and ideology of authors such as Geoffrey Scott, John Summerson and Peter Collins. But if analogy works like a cultural operator to grasp reality, we might characterize the architects presented here with specific themes that reveal their individual paths and guide us in the meanderings of contemporary architecture in Québec. These themes are carriers of a "sharing of senses."[12] They catalyze not only the interpretation of the situation and development of the architectural project that the building expresses, but offer a kind of deep structure for this sharing. The building is both a mechanism and a sign of hospitality, renewing again and again the possibility of inventing a common world. It might also be possible to say that this sensory reasoning opens onto a critical construction of reality. Each of the architects presented in this exhibition makes a contribution to moving beyond modernism according to his or her conceptual model and ethic. In this way, different analogical thoughts coexist and create a particular reality: Dan Hanganu's approach is scholastic and connected to craft, atelier big city's is friendly and playful, Saucier + Perrotte's is tactile and scenographic, Éric Gauthier's and FABG's is tectonic, while atelier TAG is topographic and Pierre Thibault's is narrative and mythical. They all choose different paths to achieve substance in their works.

Thus, at the turn of the century in our democratic society, the architect is finally free, just as Melvin Charney wished; free to create real and potential relationships through architecture for others. In Québec, however, this freedom seems to be contested in the name of public interest. Clients increasingly look for proposals that are risk-free. What will architects do then, when experimentation is eradicated from their work? Architecture in Québec, distanced from power, has never been so close to politics.

12. Jacques Rancière, *Le partage du sensible: Esthétique et politique* (Paris: La Fabrique, 2000), n.p..

GEORGES ADAMCZYK is professor and head of the School of Architecture at the University of Montréal; previously, he was professor in the Department of Design of the University of Québec at Montréal beginning in 1977. From 1992 to 1999, he was the director of the Design Centre at UQAM, a gallery dedicated to exhibitions and discussions on the city, architecture, landscape, design and graphic media. He is co-founder of *SILO*, an architectural review published by STUDIO CUBE, a group of Québec professionals and academics dedicated to the heritage of the modern architecture movement, and is a member of the editorial board of *ARQ: Architecture Québec*. He is also the author of numerous articles, communications, publications, and exhibitions; his latest contribution appears in the book *Architectural Installations* (Canadian Centre for Architecture, 1999). He organized the 1998 exhibition and edited the 2004 catalogue of *Maisons-Lieux/Houses-Places* for the Biennale de Montréal, and guest curated the exhibition *Objets trouvés* installed by Saucier + Perrotte at the Canadian Pavilion of the Venice Biennale in 2004.

Jacques Rousseau, Maison Coloniale, Montréal

Kuwabara Payne McKenna Blumberg, Kitchener City Hall

MANNERED MODERNISM: FIFTEEN YEARS OF CANADIAN ARCHITECTURE
Marco Polo

MODERNISM: REDISCOVERY AND REHABILITATION

The late 1980s were a time of considerable critical ferment in Canadian architecture. A number of phenomena emerged around this time that informed architectural practice and production over the past fifteen years. Among these was the re-emergence of an interest in Modern architecture as a source for formal inspiration. Reaching Canada later than Europe and the United States, postmodern historicism had a short but intense run in the 1980s during the brief interregnum between the dominance of late modernism in the 1960s and 1970s and the mannered modernism typical of contemporary practice since 1990.

Among the critical activities marking this pivotal moment was the touring exhibition, *A Measure of Consensus: Canadian Architecture in Transition*, curated by Andrew Gruft and shown in Vancouver, New York, Toronto and Montréal between February 1986 and April 1987. The exhibition sought to identify and set in critical context a number of developments that distinguished Canadian architecture of the early 1980s from the work of the previous generation, characterized by what could loosely be called late modernism. This idiom, which dominated the work of the 1960s and 1970s and has been referred to by Peter Buchanan as the "heroic" period of Canadian architecture,[1] was typified by large-scale interventions often on remote sites and showing little interest in history, urban context or spatial and material complexity, opting instead for bold ("heroic") gestures set in relation to majestic landscapes. Familiar examples include Erickson/Massey's Simon Fraser University in Vancouver (1965) and John Andrews' Scarborough College on the outskirts of Toronto (1964).

A Measure of Consensus identified twenty-one projects conceived between 1980 and 1984 (several never realized) that represented a renewed interest in precisely

1. Peter Buchanan, "Back to the Future," *Canadian Architect*, vol. 39, no. 3 (March 1994), 22.

those concerns unexplored in late Modern works: history, urbanity, spatial and material complexity. Although the catalogue text deliberately avoided dubbing the new work "postmodern," most of the exhibited projects adopted expressive strategies consistent with that movement: an interest in formal typology, historic precedent, complexity and contradiction, irony and fragmentation. The avoidance of stylistic terminology is significant: rather than being considered from the perspective of aesthetics, these strategies or concerns were examined as principles underlying a new sensibility that distinguished the projects from the work of a generation earlier. In fact, some of the projects included in the exhibition could be seen, in formal terms, as early harbingers of the Modern revival to come: Baird Sampson Neuert's submission to the Edmonton City Hall Competition of 1980 and Peter Cardew's Expo 86 Tower, designed in 1984 for the Vancouver world exposition, addressed many of the tendencies described in the exhibition, including an interest in history, but in the context of modernism. Baird Sampson Neuert explored the possibilities of a fragmented Modern vocabulary for civic architecture, and Cardew's tower referred to the tradition of techno-fetishism of symbolic monuments at World's Fairs in general (Paxton's Crystal Palace in London, 1851; Eiffel's Tower in Paris, 1889; A. + J. Polak's and Waterkeyn's Atomium in Brussels, 1958; Buckminster Fuller's geodesic United States Pavilion in Montréal, 1967), and to El Lissitzky's *Lenin Tribune* in particular.

The re-emergence of modernism as the *Lingua Franca* of contemporary architecture prefigured by these projects was fuelled by a number of phenomena. In the Canadian context, by the mid-1980s a new generation of architects and critics had begun to challenge what had devolved into knee-jerk critiques of modernism and sought to set the work in a more rigorous critical context. In 1985, Marc Baraness, Ruth Cawker, George Kapelos, Detlef Mertins and Brigitte Shim established the Bureau of Architecture and Urbanism (BAU), primarily in response to the demolition of George A. Robb's 1955 The Shell Oil Tower (also known as the Bulova Tower) on Toronto's Canadian National Exhibition grounds. In 1987, BAU assembled the exhibition and publication *Toronto Modern: Architecture, 1945-1965*.[2]

While BAU's focus was on manifestations of modernism specific to Toronto, the impulse to rehabilitate the much-maligned Modern movement was part of an international phenomenon that simmered beneath the surface of the dominant historicist doctrine of the time (the International Working Party for the Documentation and Conservation of Buildings, Sites and Neighbourhoods of the Modern Movement—DoCoMoMo—was established in the Netherlands in 1988). Despite the dominant polemic of the early 1980s that defined modernism as a

A Measure of Consensus, catalogue cover

2. Marc Baraness, Ruth Cawker, George Kapelos, Detlef Mertins and Brigitte Shim, eds. *Toronto Modern: Architecture 1945-1965* (Toronto: Coach House Press, 1987).

3. Tom Wolfe, *From Bauhaus to Our House* (New York: Farrar, Straus, Giroux, 1981).

4. Mark Wigley and Philip Johnson, *Deconstructivist Architecture* (New York: Museum of Modern Art, 1988).

5. Mary McLeod, "Architecture and Politics in the Reagan Era: From Postmodernism to Deconstructivism," *Assemblage* 8 (February 1989). Reprinted in *Architecture Theory Since 1968*, K. Michael Hays, ed. (Cambridge: The MIT Press, 1998), 691.

6. Wigley and Johnson, 11.

failed experiment in social engineering, even subjected to ridicule in popular criticism like Tom Wolfe's *From Bauhaus to Our House*,[3] dissenting voices were laying the groundwork for the return of a more nuanced understanding of Modern architecture. Throughout the 1980s a number of critical practices engaged in a critique of mainstream modernism, but resisted the popular tendency of reverting to nostalgic historicism, using instead the formal language of modernism to challenge and subvert the original movement's tenets. Peter Eisenman's and Richard Trott's Wexner Center for the Performing Arts in Columbus, Ohio (1989), Zaha Hadid's winning submission to the Peak International Design Competition for Hong Kong (1983), Rem Koolhaas/OMA's proposal for an Observation Tower, Rotterdam (1982), Coop Himmelb(l)au's rooftop remodelling Falkestraße in Vienna (1985), and the widely published early 1980s work of a fledgling Morphosis in Los Angeles were all Modern in expression, but adopted a some-times ambivalent, sometimes pointedly critical position with regard to modernism's technological determinism and utopianism.

Like postmodern historicism, this work—much of which was included in *Deconstructivist Architecture*,[4] the 1988 publication and exhibition at the Museum of Modern Art, curated by Mark Wigley and Philip Johnson—borrowed forms and images from the past, but it did so in a rhetorical and critical way. Where it differed from its formal predecessors was in its rejection of "the fundamental ideological premises of the Modern movement: functionalism, structural ration-alism and a faith in social regeneration."[5] Where modernism was totalizing, Deconstructivism was atomizing; where modernism celebrated faith in progress and technology, embracing an agenda of emancipation through mechanization, Deconstructivism expressed uncertainty and instability; where modernism sought formal purity, Deconstructivism identified, using the language of psychoanalysis, "the symptoms of a repressed impurity"[6]; where modernism sought to establish a new cultural order through a process of standardization and rationalization, Deconstructivism expressed idiosyncrasy, disjunction and disorder.

The critical activity of the 1980s had a profound influence on Canadian archi-tecture. In 1989, the city of Kitchener, Ontario launched a national competition for the design of a new city hall. What emerged from that competition was a rich response to the complex and contradictory forces influencing architecture on the cusp of the 1990s: a renewed interest in the forms of modernism, tempered by history, urbanity, and spatial and material complexity, forces that would inform the work of a new generation of Modern revivalists.

Kitchener City Hall competition entries (clockwise from left)
Saucier + Perrotte, Dunlop Architects, Kohn Shnier, Teeple Architects

A NEW MANNERISM: CANADIAN ARCHITECTURE IN THE 1990s

Edward Jones' and Michael Kirkland's Mississauga City Hall—arguably the apogee of postmodern architecture in Canada—was completed in 1986 only to have its embrace of Krier's neoclassicism trumped three years later by the five finalists in the Kitchener City Hall competition. Kuwabara Payne McKenna Blumberg Architects' (KPMB) winning submission to that competition—selected by a jury composed of architects Alan Colquhoun, Richard Henriquez and Peter Rose, and citizens Jan Ciuciura and Beverley Hummitzsch under the guidance of profess-ional advisor Detlef Mertins—proposed a dramatic departure from the nostalgic historicism that characterized much of the architecture of the previous decade, re-establishing modernism as a legitimate idiom for major civic buildings. What's more, this strategy was not exclusive to the winning scheme: other finalists in the Kitchener competition included submissions by Kohn Shnier, Dunlop Architects, Teeple Architects and Saucier + Perrotte, all of which foretold the Modern revival of the 1990s. Their choice of architectural expression left little doubt that post-modern classicism was about to be replaced by the modernist language of an emerging generation of practices that now number among Canada's most celebrated firms.

7. Larry Richards, "Reworking Modernism," *Competing Visions: The Kitchener City Hall Competition*, Detlef Mertins and Virginia Wright, eds. (Toronto: The Melting Press, 1990), 115-127.

8. Kenneth Frampton, "Intimate Monumentality," *Canadian Architect*, vol. 39, no. 7 (July 1994), 18.

9. John Fleming, Hugh Honour and Niklaus Pevsner, *The Penguin Dictionary of Architecture and Landscape Architecture*, Fifth Edition (London: Penguin Books, 1999), 361.

In his essay "Reworking Modernism,"[7] Larry Richards identifies numerous sources that are legible in the five finalist schemes. What emerges as most significant is not any one particular source, but the wide range of influences that Richards enumerates. In the case of KPMB's winning submission, these range from Walter Gropius to Morphosis to Ivan Leonidov to James Stirling—as well as George Robb's recently demolished Bulova Tower—attesting to the eclectic revivalism imbedded beneath its modernist skin. Writing about the project in *Canadian Architect*, Kenneth Frampton described the project as seeking "to evoke through superimposition a loose conjunction of two categorically opposed values; one a modernity that is high-tech in its aspirations…the other the evocation of traditional institutional form."[8]

In its broad and studied eclecticism, Kitchener City Hall has more in common with the work of the early 1980s identified in *A Measure of Consensus* than it does with its Modern progenitors: an interest in urbanism, in history (albeit more recent history), complexity and materiality. This is true of the Modern revival ushered in by the competition and which characterizes much of the work of the past fifteen years. It appears in retrospect that the elements and preoccupations identified in *A Measure of Consensus* did indeed transcend style and expression, defining a set of concerns and strategies that differentiate the more recent work from its Modern forebears.

What all of this suggests is the emergence of a mannered modernism; one that adopts the formal properties of the Modern, but that treats expression as a rhetorical device rather than a resultant of more rational or functionalist design strategies. In *The Penguin Dictionary of Architecture and Landscape Architecture*, John Fleming, Hugh Honour and Nikolaus Pevsner define Mannerism as "characterized by the use of motifs in deliberate opposition to their original significance or context."[9] This can be applied to much of the work of the past fifteen years that, while Modern in expression, is distinguished from post-war modernism in much the same way that Mannerist architecture was both an offshoot of and reaction against the orthodoxies of Renaissance classicism, adopting similar formal motifs but tending to subjective interpretation and aestheticization. Sixteenth century Mannerism adopted the formal language of the Renaissance, but remained aloof from its humanist underpinnings; recent architecture adopts the aesthetic of modernism, but not its interest in standardization and mechanization or its underlying utopian agenda. The Modern aesthetic is decontextualized from the socio-political and economic conditions from which it originally emerged, and recontextualized, if not in "deliberate opposition to its original significance," then at least in a milieu where it is valued not as an agent of cultural change, not as a means to an end, but as an end in itself.

Mary McLeod has suggested that such a retreat from the social dimension of modernism is consistent with the broader neo-conservative tendency of the 1980s and early 1990s, expressed in architectural terms by a fascination with "surface, image and play" and, significantly, the abandonment of "housing as a social program."[10] This is amply illustrated in the Canadian experience, whereby the mid-1990s the federal government and all provincial governments save those of British Columbia and Québec had discontinued their involvement in the provision of affordable housing, once a mainstay of Modern architectural practice and a primary beneficiary of strategies of standardization and mass production, as illustrated by the success of the *Slesia Siedlungen* projects (1919-1925) carried out in Germany between the wars. According to McLeod, the commodification of architectural image ushered in by postmodernism has persisted in the recent wave of Modern revivalism, robbing the aesthetic of its original encoded meaning.

10. McLeod, 682.

Some of this work has come to define a particular idiom in contemporary Canadian architecture identified by Calgary architect Marc Boutin as "Comfy Modernism."[11] In his role as a jury member for the 2003 Canadian Architect Awards of Excellence, Boutin wrote that this idiom has become "Canadian architecture's *de facto* style...and though it can be characterized as an extremely competent, formally sophisticated version of modernism, it is ultimately a soft echo of its heroic ancestry, and more closely associated with Philip Johnson [Henry-Russell Hitchcock] and Alfred Barr's liquidation of modern architecture through the stylistic concerns defined in their *International Style*."[12]

11. Marc Boutin, *Canadian Architect*, vol. 48, no. 12 (December 2003), 10.

12. Ibid., 10-11.

While Boutin is clearly critical of the current work's renouncement of modernism's ambition to act as harbinger of social and cultural change, others see this as an expression of modesty befitting architecture's role in contemporary society. In the November 6, 2004, edition of *The Globe and Mail*, Lisa Rochon wrote glowingly of the "new modernism that's defining the public and private face of Toronto," and argued that it "has an agenda: humanizing the strict religion of modern architecture," resulting in "architecture that is human-sized, human-complex, human-warm,"[13] or as Boutin might say, "comfy."

13. Lisa Rochon, *The Globe and Mail*, November 6, 2004, M4.

It's tempting to characterize the current work as resulting from the *strict religion of modern architecture* being tempered by an injection of phenomenology and postmodern humanism. However, as Rochon rightly points out, despite her own characterization of the work as "new modernism" this tendency is not altogether new, borrowing and extending formal themes developed by an earlier generation of architects. A similar hybrid condition already existed in Canadian Modern architecture. Indeed, it is possible to see how preoccupations in current Canadian architecture can be traced back to the early post-war period, when two distinct streams of modernism emerged. One stream—the one championed by Rochon and critiqued by Boutin—can be described as romantic, experiential, picturesque and idiosyncratic, influenced by Frank Lloyd Wright, Alvar Aalto and Louis Kahn, with Ron Thom and a current generation of admirers, including Toronto's Shim-Sutcliffe Architects and Ian MacDonald Architect, and Vancouver's Patkau Architects, among its Canadian proponents. Characterized by a high degree of specificity, this work maintains a keen interest in materiality and tactility, as well as a strong relationship to site and context. In many respects, this work is consistent with Kenneth Frampton's notion of "Critical Regionalism" first articulated in 1982, which argued from a phenomenological concern for place-making that architecture "find its governing inspiration in such things as the range and quality of the local light, or in a *tectonic* derived from a peculiar structural mode, or in the topography of a given site."[14] In more extreme examples, overt interest in materiality, tectonics and fetishistic attention to detail seem to be pursued as ends in themselves; the architecture derives its meaning from its material manifestation. To borrow terminology from existential philosophy, in this work, existence precedes essence.

The other stream—decidedly less *comfy*—can be understood as more conceptually than phenomenologically driven, with its primary influences coming from Mies van der Rohe and Walter Gropius. Less widely disseminated in Canada than the first stream, it is more typical of contemporary international work, particularly Dutch Supermodernism, and finds expression in the work of Montréal-based Saucier + Perrotte architectes, among others. It is characterized by an emphasis on the visual rather than the tactile, spatial and material ambiguity, dematerialization and transparency (increasingly reflecting the influence of new digital media, used as tools for design, as well as representation) and exhibits an interest in the universal rather than the particular. In spite of their relative aloofness to tactility, the most successful examples also exhibit skilful manipulation of materiality and detail, treated not as ends within themselves, but as phenomenal manifestations of more abstract conceptual ideas. Here, essence precedes existence.

The work of the past fifteen years has continued to develop themes embodied in these two divergent tendencies in Canadian post-war architecture. In both

14. Kenneth Frampton, "Towards a Critical Regionalism: Six Points for an Architecture of Resistance," *The Anti-Aesthetic: Essays on Postmodern Culture*. Hal Foster, ed. (Port Townsend: Bay Press, 1983), 21.

cases, recent works represent mannered versions of the originals they emulate, manifesting what Larry Richards has called the "capacity of twentieth century modernism to be transformed and to adjust to contemporary needs and aspirations."[15] In addition, many of the themes explored in this work are similar to those that informed the projects examined in *A Measure of Consensus*—history, urbanity and spatial and material complexity—but all within the formal language of modernism.

15. Richards, 127.

CONSENSUS AND CONTINUITY: ISSUES IN CANADIAN PRACTICE

That many of the underlying themes informing recent work have remained consistent since the late 1980s should not be altogether surprising, since many of the architects whose work was represented in *A Measure of Consensus* continue to occupy important positions within Canadian practice, and appear again in the 2005 exhibition, *Substance Over Spectacle: Contemporary Canadian Architecture*. Of the twenty-one architects or firms represented in the 1986 exhibition, eight are included in the new show, and several on the current list were members of design teams on projects included in *A Measure of Consensus*. This suggests considerable continuity within Canadian architectural practice over the past fifteen to twenty years, a situation reflected in the relatively small number of architects in the country and the much smaller circle whose work is recognized as exemplary. Commenting on this phenomenon in his capacity as a jury member for the 2000 *Canadian Architect* Awards of Excellence, Vancouver architect, John Patkau, noted that "The architects of these projects are the relatively small group of slowly changing usual suspects."[16] While holding the profession ultimately responsible for the cultivation of the discipline and the pursuit of opportunity for young practitioners, Patkau also argued that part of the blame rested "with the bankruptcy of cultural leadership in the public sector."[17] This is of particular significance to Canadian architects, as the public sector maintains a very robust presence in the construction industry, particularly with respect to architectural services. In 1999, institutional projects constituted just over 10 percent of total construction value in Canada, but accounted for almost 40 percent of architectural fees, mostly from projects related to health care and education.[18]

16. John Patkau, *Canadian Architect*, vol. 45, no. 12 (December 2000), 14.

17. Ibid.

18. Statistics Canada, http://www.statcan.ca/Daily/English/030416/dD30416F.htm.

Patkau argues that a significant problem lies with the procurement process typically used for such projects: "our failure to develop the use of mechanisms other than practice experience checklists for selecting architects has resulted in an almost impenetrable glass ceiling for talented young architects."[19] Young designers

19. Patkau, 14.

20. McGill Business Consulting Group, "Succeeding by Design: A Perspective on Strengthening the Profession of Architecture in Ontario and Canada," *Ontario Association of Architects* (Montréal: McGill Business Consulting Group, 2003).

seeking the opportunity to work on these prestigious and challenging projects often have little choice but to seek employment with the few firms that have a chance at procuring them. One result of this phenomenon seems to be the declining number of licensed architects in this country. "Succeeding by Design,"[20] a study prepared in 2003 by the McGill Business Consulting Group for four provincial associations and the Royal Architectural Institute of Canada, noted this decline even in the past few years despite a concurrent increase in construction activity (the value of building permits issued in Canada ballooned from $35.7 billion in 1999 to $50.7 billion in 2003—an increase of 42 percent).

The study suggests that this decline can, in part, be accounted for by the fact that architectural practices are getting larger, absorbing many young designers seeking the opportunity to work on significant institutional projects. Working within companies with licensed senior architects, young employees may not feel compelled to undertake the onerous process of completing their professional registration. In recent years an even more extreme form of this phenomenon has seen the absorption of already substantial architectural practices by large international firms, in some instances by engineering giants. Alberta-based Stantec has led the pack in this respect, absorbing several large firms in British Columbia and Alberta, recently moving into Ontario with the acquisition of Dunlop Architects; Vancouver's Busby + Associates recently merged with the large American firm Perkins + Will to become Busby, Perkins + Will; some years ago Toronto's Urbana Architects joined forces with HOK (Hellmuth, Obata + Kassabaum). These alliances represent a significant concentration of expertise and resources, establishing strategic positions within the competitive marketplace.

An alternative route for young architects has been the establishment of "boutique" practices, which develop work of very high quality and architectural ambition, but rarely find the opportunity to expand beyond the design of custom houses. This is increasingly not only an issue of opportunity; there are significant institutional obstacles complicating the transition from boutique residential practice, among them the difficulty and expense of obtaining liability insurance for larger projects. All these forces contribute to what the McGill Report identified as the increasing polarization of practice between larger firms with established practice infrastructure and smaller firms, which place an emphasis on small-scale, highly customized design projects.

An offshoot of these two extremes of practice that has proliferated over the last decade is the joint venture, in which firms pool their disparate talents in order to secure work that they might not otherwise have access to. This often involves the partnering of smaller firms with strong reputations for design excellence and larger firms with expertise in building technology and project delivery that inspire confidence in a potentially skittish client. Increasingly, these joint ventures are bringing together firms from different regions of the country seeking opportunities beyond those available to them in local markets.

The attempt to reach beyond local markets became increasingly important over the past fifteen years, as firms sought to overcome a debilitating cycle of boom and bust that plagued local economies across the country. As a result, architects who successfully pursued opportunities in regions other than their own established practices that are now national in scope. Despite the return in the late 1990s of buoyant economies throughout much of the country, these practices continue to serve national and in some cases international markets, routinely working in other regions of the country. Finally, the re-emergence of Montréal, since the late 1990s, as a centre of architectural activity after a generation of economic dormancy is especially interesting: eight of ten projects recognized in last year's *Canadian Architect* Awards of Excellence were designed by Québec architects. In addition, opportunities in that city for architects from other parts of the country—such as the Patkaus, Busby, Perkins + Will and KPMB—and three recent projects in Ontario by Saucier + Perrotte of Montréal (the Perimeter Institute in Waterloo, New College Student Residence at the University of Toronto St. George Campus and CCIT at the University of Toronto in Mississauga) suggest interesting possibilities for cross-fertilization and fostering the development of architectural sensibilities that challenge the mannered regionalism that dominated the 1990s.

CODA: MODERNISM, ONCE MORE, WITH FEELING

In his essay "Reworking Modernism," Larry Richards notes that "Architecture produces architecture: that is the nature of its history."[21] This was especially true when he wrote it in 1990; architecture was in the thick of an obsessive self-referentiality, struggling to come to terms with its turbulent recent history and find renewed meaning and social relevance. The resulting irony of the 1990s was the use of modernism, founded on the rejection of the historicism of the nineteenth century, as a mannered historic style.

21. Richards, 123.

But it is not just architecture that produces architecture. In *Vers une Architecture*, Le Corbusier cautioned that "The lesson of the airplane is not primarily in the forms it has created, and above all we must learn to see in an airplane not a bird or a

22. Le Corbusier, *Towards a New Architecture* (New York: Dover, 1986), 110.

dragonfly, but a machine for flying; the lesson of the airplane lies in the logic that governed the enunciation of the problem and which led to its successful realization. When a problem is properly stated, in our epoch, it inevitably finds its solution."[22] The late 1980s not only brought a high degree of critical ferment to architecture, but gave birth to a variety of initiatives that have sought to properly state a problem and that have gradually come to influence architectural practice. In 1987, while architectural culture was largely consumed by issues of formalism, the United Nations Commission on Environment and Development led by former Norwegian Prime Minister Grø Harlem Brundtland published *Our Common Future*. The Brundtland Report has turned out to be a foundation manifesto of sorts for the sustainability movement, defining the deleterious environmental impact of conventional models of development and calling for "a form of sustainable development which meets the needs of the present without compromising the ability of future generations to meet their own needs."[23]

23. World Commission on Environment and Development, *Our Common Future* (London: Oxford, 1987), 8.

After toiling on the sidelines of critical discourse in architecture for the better part of a decade, the pursuit of sustainability suggests the possibility of a fundamental shift in architectural priorities. If the architecture of the last fifteen years has displayed a tendency to mannered formalism, the imperatives of sustainable design suggest a return to other aspects of the Modern movement, namely its instrumentalist roots, putting technology at the service of a larger social agenda and confirming the "capacity of twentieth century modernism to be transformed and to adjust to contemporary needs and aspirations."[24] Having focused on the formal aspects of modernism, architects may yet have lessons to learn from other dimensions of the Modern movement and reclaim a more direct and engaged level of social relevance.

24. Richards, 127.

MARCO POLO is a graduate of the University of British Columbia School of Architecture. After completing his studies in 1985 he relocated to Toronto, where he spent the next twelve years in full-time professional practice. He is a registered architect with the Ontario Association of Architects (OAA) and a member of the Royal Architectural Institute of Canada (RAIC). He has written extensively on architecture for *Canadian Architect, Azure, The Globe and Mail*, and *Insite*. In 1997, he became editor of *Canadian Architect* magazine, where he remained as Editorial Director until 2003. He has also served as guest critic at the Universities of British Columbia, Calgary, Manitoba, Waterloo, and Dalhousie. He has been teaching since 1996, and in 2002 was appointed Assistant Professor in Ryerson University's Department of Architectural Science in Toronto, where his teaching focus is in architecture theory and the design studio.

SUBSTANCE OVER SPECTACLE
Essays copyright © 2005 by the Contributors

All rights reserved. No part of this book may be reproduced or used
in any form by any means—graphic, electronic or mechanical—without
the prior written permission of the publisher, except by a reviewer,
who may use brief excerpts in a review, or in the case of photocopy-
ing in Canada, a license from the Canadian Copyright Licensing Agency.

ARSENAL PULP PRESS
103-1014 Homer Street
Vancouver, BC
www.arsenalpulp.com
Canada V6B 2W9

MORRIS AND HELEN BELKIN ART GALLERY
1825 Main Mall
University of British Columbia
Vancouver, BC
Canada V6T 1Z2
www.belkin-gallery.ubc.ca

Arsenal Pulp Press gratefully acknowledges the support of the Canada
Council for the Arts and the British Columbia Arts Council for its pub-
lishing programme, and the Government of Canada through the Book
Publishing Industry Development Program for its publishing activities.

The Morris and Helen Belkin Art Gallery gratefully acknowledges the
support of the Morris and Helen Belkin Endowment for Exhibitions and
Acquisitions, and our generous donors: Anonymous; Haywood
Securities Inc.; Anthony von Mandl, Proprietor, Mission Hill Family Estate;
Context Development Inc.; The Architectural Institute of British Columbia.

Book design Robin Mitchell for Picnic
Copy editor Cindy Richmond
Translation (Georges Adamczyk text) Zoe Blowen-Ledoux
Printed and bound in Canada by Hemlock Printers Ltd.

Front cover image Strawberry Vale Elementary School
Photo by James Dow
Back cover image Perimeter Institute
Photo by Marc Cramer
Last page image atelier big city, Bourg de Pabos

LIBRARY AND ARCHIVES CANADA
IN PUBLICATION
Gruft, Andrew
        Substance over spectacle : contemporary Canadian architecture
/ Andrew Gruft.

Published to coincide with the eponymous exhibition, mounted by the
Morris and Helen Belkin Art Gallery at the University of British
Columbia, April 2005.
Co-published by the Morris and Helen Belkin Art Gallery.
Includes bibliographical references and index.
ISBN 1-55152-185-7

        1. Architecture, Modern—Canada—20th century—Exhibitions.
I. Morris and Helen Belkin Art Gallery II. Title.
NA745.6.G78 2005   720'.971'07471133   C2005-901432-6

Canada, I think I love you, but I wanna know for sure.
— Apologies to the Troggs

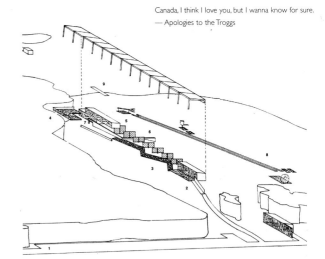